Theoretical

Perspectives in

Architectural

History and

Criticism

Mark Rakatansky, Series Editor

Jennifer Bloomer

Architecture and the Text: The (S)crypts of Joyce and Piranesi

Yale University Press

New Haven and London

Published with assistance from the foundation established in memory of
Amasa Stone Mather of the Class of 1907, Yale College.

Designed by Sylvia Steiner.
Set in Gill Sans Condensed and Sabon type by Tseng Information Systems,
Inc., Durham, North Carolina.
Printed in the United States of America by Vail-Ballou Press, Binghamton,
New York.

Library of Congress Cataloging-in-Publication Data

Bloomer, Jennifer.
Architecture and the text : the (s)crypts of Joyce and Piranesi / Jennifer
Bloomer.
p.   cm. — (Theoretical perspectives in architectural history and
criticism)
Includes bibliographical references and index.
ISBN 0-300-04927-7 (cloth)
        0-300-06302-4 (pbk.)
1. Signs and symbols in architecture.   2. Architecture—Philosophy.
I. Title.   II. Series.
NA2500.B57   1993
720'.1—dc20   92-31624 CIP

A catalogue record for this book is available from the British Library.

10   9   8   7   6   5   4   3   2

For Bob

Contents

A Beginning

The generative seed of this book is, like Louis Sullivan's seedpod or Euclid's *vesica piscis* diagram of two intersecting circles, bilobate. Each lobe developed out of a moment when I was a student, sitting in a classroom and feeling utterly perplexed.

The first moment occurred in 1969 at Mount Holyoke College. I was seventeen, fresh from a public high school in East Tennessee where girls were discouraged from wearing trousers or displaying intelligence, and I was bewildered. The jeans-and-work-shirt-cum-peace-symbol environment of South Hadley was one thing. But Miss Adelaide Potter's assignment of the "Anna Livia" section of *Finnegans Wake* was quite another. We were actually expected to be able to talk about this impenetrable piece of garbage on Monday? Although Miss Potter's beautiful reading and decoding on Monday failed to draw me further into the text, it planted half a seed. Years later as a student in architecture school, I would run across Bernard Tschumi's assertion that *Finnegans Wake* was one of the greatest works of twentieth-century architecture. In frustration, I dug out my old book, determined to discover what he meant by that. I walked in, and didn't come out for years, until I had come to terms with Joyce.

The second lobe grew out of a later time and out of a specific question: How do I come to terms with Piranesi, who won't leave me alone, who is always turning up—in the picture gallery at Soane's house; in the cool, dark halls of Girton College, Cambridge, during my blissful, solitary summer there; on the walls of Morrison's Cafeteria in Atlanta; at the foot of the stairs the first time and every time I visit my mother-in-law's house in Athens, Georgia. Old, baffling Piranesi, who, in the 1750 Polanzani portrait, where he appears without clothing and with his right arm broken off like an antique statue, looks so like my husband (and our infant daughter) that it makes us laugh. It was my husband who first introduced me to Piranesi. He wasn't my husband then; he was my teacher. My teacher, then my colleague, then my lover, then my husband, then the father of my daughter. I shall be his widow. When that time comes, the cheap Piranesis—the strange bits that nobody else wants and that we love, that we forage for in musty old shops—will hang around and be part of his ghost.

When I was a student in Professor Segrest's urban design class in architecture school, he flashed up a slide of the *Campo Marzio* and made remarks about the brilliance of Piranesi and his plans of Rome and then went on to something else. The jerk. I distinctly remember sitting there thinking I was the only person in the large class who didn't understand this Piranesi stuff and who didn't understand that whatever it was about his work that was so brilliant was so self-evident that it required no professorial explanation whatsoever. As Professor Segrest now knows only too well, things stick in my craw; and so I have tortured him with Piranesi for years. As this book nears completion, I consider us almost even.

Like the two parts of the *vesica piscis,* the lobes of Joyce and Piranesi share a lot of territory. That is what my text, a woven object, is about: the spaces between things. This book is also a puzzle and, like a puzzle, it is meant to be difficult and challenging, but fun. These chapters were, in fact, written out of a frustration with attempts to describe in a linear fashion what architects do when we design. I have tried here to demonstrate an approach to design rather than to explain it in a scientific fashion. I wrote the book around and for my students, especially for those who understand that architecture is a beautifully broad and deep discipline as well as a profession, and, even more especially, for those who do not. It is full of convention, invention, critique, sly allusion, geometry, and stuff from the heart, as all architecture should be. I hope it gives some pleasure.

The temporal boundaries of the book are the emergences of my two daughters into the world of language. Two offspring, two mirror encounters: a familiar motif. As Sarah Elizabeth began to utter, it began; and now, eleven years later, as Laura Barrett demands the breast to appear with her "mamama" and her astonishing thunderwords, it ends. With talking come dreams. The body makes constructions of desire with words as stuff. It begins again.

Upon completion, 13 January 1992
(1.13.'2)
The day Joyce died, 51 years after.

Acknowledgments

A lot of people have done me many kindnesses over the production of this work. There is not enough space to name them all, but there are some special thank-yous to be made:

To Ken Knoespel, Angel Medina, John Archea, and Marco Frascari, for shepherding me through the long phase when this book was a dissertation.

To Greg Ulmer, whose work was there in the beginning and whose friendship was there in the end.

To Guy Davenport, for writing, for writing back, and for sharing his mind.

To Jacques Derrida, for kind words of encouragement and for patiently listening to me when neither of us knew what I was talking about.

To two living fathers who take the heat, as well as the gratitude for the legacy: Peter Eisenman and Manfredo Tafuri.

To my academic siblings: Ann Bergren, Beatriz Colomina, Michael Hays, Catherine Ingraham, Jeff Kipnis, and Mark Wigley, for input, feedback, appropriations, encouragement, warm feelings, and big phone bills.

To my students at Georgia Tech and the University of Florida, who helped make my studios and seminars productive toward this end. Especially Durham Crout and Mikesch Muecke, two who really challenged me and who remain friends.

To two wonder women at Yale University Press: Senior Editor Judy Metro, for her enthusiastic support of this project, and Manuscript Editor

Susan Laity, for whipping a flabby manuscript into shape with her impressive mix of knowledge, competence, and good humor. And to Mark Rakatansky, Series Editor, who had faith in this book.

To my children: Sarah Elizabeth Cox, Taylor Segrest, and Laura Barrett Bloomer-Segrest, but especially to Sarah, whose entire post-toddler life has been backgrounded by this thing. For keeping me connected to what it's really all about.

To my husband, Robert Segrest. For unwavering generosity, patience, and presence.

A Priming

To concentrate solely on the literal sense or even the psychological content of any document to the sore neglect of the enveloping facts themselves circumstantiating it is just as hurtful to sound sense. . . . Who in his heart doubts either that the facts of feminine clothiering are there all the time or that the feminine fiction, stranger than the facts, is there also at the same time, only a little to the rere? Or that one may be separated from the other? Or that both may then be contemplated simultaneously? Or that each may be taken up and considered in turn apart from the other?
Finnegans Wake 109.12–36

The letter! The litter! And the soother the bitther! Of eyebrow pencilled, by lipstipple penned.
Finnegans Wake 93.24–25

All conventional scholarly work ("original research") is written in the implied first person. Under the mask of objectivity, "I am interested in" becomes "The focus of this study is." The following chapters make no pretense at objectivity: they represent the residue of my self, my cultural condition, my passion (love and hate) for architecture. The non-neutrality of language and history (and architecture) are my concerns. To situate this work in an epistemological arena that relies upon the maintenance of belief in their transparencies would be an error of logic. It cannot be written otherwise. It is, therefore, written other-wise.

This text (in the territory beyond this prim[p]ing) consists of an introduction, which is an allegorical construction on allegory, a collection of three-plus-one essays upon some etchings of Giambattista Piranesi, and an appendix that serves as a guide to variant readings. There is in the construction a double, slipping structure of the three-plus-one configuration: chapters 1, 2, and 3 constitute a threesome, with the fourth chapter—chapter 3-plus-one (the *Syllapsies*)—as the "plus-one"; and the three constructions within chapter 2 constitute a threesome, with chapter 3 ("The House That Jack Built") as construction 3-plus-one. In both cases the "plus-one" is both excessive (an addition to that which might already be considered complete) and completing (an addition that points to the incompleteness of the three at hand). The number three, the number three-plus-one, and the sum of these two numbers form the dominant numerical armature of the book. The strategies for writing/constructing/reading this work are appropriated from strategies dissected out of the text of James Joyce's *Finnegans Wake*.

Piranesi was an eighteenth-century architect known primarily for his voluminous etchings, slightly less for his treatise on architecture, and much less for his built work. Nevertheless he was all that the above suggest: recorder, visionary, theoretician, and practitioner. His oeuvre in many respects is painfully out of synchronization with the conventions of his time and place, and some of the work has been interpreted as bizarre and delirium-produced. He has been called the first modern architect. To classify Piranesi is, of course, absurd. What is important is that in his portrait by Labruzzi, he is wearing a beautiful silk satin coat and a dark suede waistcoat over a shirt edged with sheer organdy ruffles freshly pressed. He sits in a pose appropriate to his position, displaying one of his drawings. But under his fingernails there is blackness.

James Joyce was a twentieth-century writer known primarily for a collection of short stories, a short novel, a masterpiece deemed obscene and banned in the United States, and a meta-masterpiece certainly much more obscene by such standards than its predecessor, but deemed unreadable and therefore not banned in the United States. His oeuvre is painfully out of synchronization with the conventions of his time and place, and some of the work has been interpreted as bizarre and delirium-produced. He has been called the greatest modern writer and the first postmodern writer. To classify Joyce is, of course, absurd. What is important is that in any of several photographs that have become our collective image of him, his eyes, magnified to fantastic proportions behind thick lenses, are unfocused and slightly crossed, a hint that they are full of darkness and shadow.

The two images, the painting of Piranesi and the photograph of Joyce, that have just been described with words do not appear in this text. Most of the images that do appear—reproductions of the etchings of Piranesi and a drawing by Joyce—are illustrations of the etchings to which the text refers; but, more important, they are emblems, or maps, for reading the allegorical text. The legibility of the image qua illustration operates only at the most mundane and even simplistic level. Piranesi's imagery should not be construed as an illustrative milieu for Joyce's visionless, in-the-dark text, but a text in images that *corresponds* to the text of words.

A primary polemic here is directed at the dominance, indeed the domination, of the image—and of the visual—in architecture and in Western culture. Thus, at the same time that this book explores the territory of the visual-image polemic, it represents a suppression of image into text, calling into question the neutrality of the image, in a move parallel to the more currently accepted recognition of the non-neutrality (transparency) of language, which, of course, is itself characterizable by a dominance of the visual.

The reader by now will have perceived that a recognition of the conventions of historiography that demand a dependence upon primary and secondary documents, upon proof of hypothesis, upon bipolar logic and hierarchical, linear thinking—that is, the conventions of research founded in what is called "scientific method"—has been abandoned. But this, to a large degree, is not true. It is not the *recognition* of scientific-method-based research that has been forsaken but blind faith in it. Conventional method is called into question here. Thus, this is a work of critical analysis that began with a constellation of questions rather than a hypothesis: Is there further research to be done on the relation between architecture and writing, research that goes beyond the pitfalls and dead ends of the arguments made over the last twenty years that depend upon semantic and syntactic translations between languages (the early architectural research of Peter Eisenman and that of Diana Agrest and Mario Gandelsonas, for example) and simple tropic analogies (the early work of Jorge Silvetti, Robert Venturi, and Michael Graves)? Where might be the sites of such relations, if not in causal correspondence? Are the configurations significant that describe the relations among language, literature, writing, drawing, building, and architecture? How might a consideration of the connections between theory and practice inform and be informed by these configurations? The relations of space and time? Those of nature and culture? If we reconstrue history and historical research in terms of a suspension of belief in the mutual exclusivity, or bipolarity, of these pairs of concepts, how might this inform and be informed by those configurations?

These questions were posed as a generative epistemological milieu from which to operate upon a set of specific texts. I chose to operate on a literary text and an architectural text that approach each other: a written text (*Finnegans Wake*) in which the writing-language-meaning relation was not displayed as transparent and univocal, and a drawn text (a collection of Piranesi's etchings—the *Campo Marzio* plan, the *Collegio,* and the *Carceri*) in which the drawing-building-meaning connection was not displayed that way. Furthermore, the texts approach each other in another way: the narrative structure of *Finnegans Wake* is superimposed upon a geometric structure that resembles an architectonic, and the Piranesi etchings approach the literary in their ambiguity and invitation to a kind of narrative interpretation (a "What is going on here?"). Both texts are presented as white pages on which black marks have been made. Both are reproduced in repetition. Both break conventions that go far beyond those of their temporal and geographical contexts, while masquerading as "normal" texts (a bound volume with title and author's name printed on the cover, pages from books about architecture), and so immediately put into disarray attempts at classification, explanation, and searches for causality.

When I use the word *writing* in this text (and I use it a lot), I do not refer simply to that concept of writing as a mirror or documentation of speech, but to writing as a constructing, nonlinear enterprise that works across culture in networks of signification. This writing, although it makes use of language, is not limited by conventional concepts of language; that is, it does not exist in identity with language.

My operation upon the texts of Joyce and Piranesi, generally speaking, uses constructive strategies found in the text of Joyce to open up the texts of Piranesi to analysis. It is no coincidence that the Joycean strategies are, to a large extent, similar to the body of contemporary critical strategies known as deconstructive.[1] In turn, the strategies of deconstruction have persuasively revealed the failures of conventional scientific method on the basis of its own logic. Therefore, a deconstructive approach seems to have an appropriate "fit" here.

The proper name most often associated with deconstructive criticism is that of Jacques Derrida, whose mode is a kind of radical empiricism. One of his most recognized signatures, the polysemous "There is nothing outside the text," suggests this regardless of how it is construed. The present work follows the lines of such empiricism; it is a close analysis of texts that at the level of material to be analyzed are closed to context and at the level of the process of analysis are open to a boundless universe of potential connectivity. The etchings of Piranesi are construed as texts in many senses. They are isolatable entities stripped of conventional contextual supports of "truth," such as biographical information about the author or relative chronological position vis à vis other texts of the author or his predecessors or contemporaries. They are readable. They are construed as "having been woven" (the word *text* emerges from the past participle of the Latin *texere*, "to weave." A text is a woven thing).

In the space of the relation between text and weaving lies the generative structure that allows the logic of the construction to unfold before your eyes. This structure must be mapped across a constellation of concepts via a network of lines of ideas that, although they may be tied to various proper names, are not purely the property of those particular proper names but, instead, represent repetitious tracks of many movements across the same territory. The proper names that follow, in other words, are in one sense coding mechanisms for the general vicinities of certain tracks. In another sense, the proper names represent a certain acquiescence to conventions of scholarship: they provide jumping off points from this work to other works that constitute its context. The mapping of this generative structure itself operates in the space between text and weaving: it is what it is about. Samuel Beckett, protégé of Joyce, said the same of *Finnegans Wake*: "Here form is content, content *is* form. You complain that this stuff is not written in English. It is not written at all. It is not to be read—or rather it is not only to be read. It is to be looked at and listened to. His writing is not *about* something; *it is that something itself*" ("Dante . . . ," *Exagmination*, 14).

Before we enter the space between text and weaving, it will be useful to explore some preliminary ("before the threshold") territory. The world in which *objectivity* and its related concepts are inscribed is a world founded in logocentrism, that is, a world in which the Divine Word of God and Its related concepts—Truth as an absolute, the centered subject, the determination of the Being as presence based in the concept of power of an inner voice, heroic and boundlessly creative subjectivity (all reflecting a need for authorization, for centeredness and a clarity of order, for control)—are operative as controlling structures.

> It is this longing for a center, an authorizing pressure, that spawns hierarchized oppositions. The superior term belongs to presence and the logos; the inferior serves to define its status and mark a fall. The oppositions between intelligible and sensible, soul and body seem to have lasted out "the history of Western philosophy," bequeathing their burden to modern linguistics' opposition between meaning and word. The opposition between writing and speech takes its place within this pattern. (Spivak, preface to Derrida, *Grammatology*, lxix).

Bipolar logic, which demands a superior and an inferior term, structures Western thought, demarcating binary categories in which one term is privileged over the other: light and darkness, male and female, theory and practice, culture and nature, creation and procreation, sacred and profane, mind and body, speech and writing.[2] In *Of Grammatology*, Derrida opens up to analysis the relation of speech and writing, exposing both the logical problems of and the motivation behind privileging speech over writing in Western culture. In *Dissemination* (and other texts), writing is set in motion; it is used as an instrument for exploring the territories of texts, marking the craters and fault lines and untrustworthy bridges that clutter texts.[3]

It has been commonly construed (especially in the architectural press) that Derrida's operation on the privileging of speech over writing is one of simple reversal, that, in fact, Derrida's "mission" is to privilege writing over speech. In architectural circles, this misconception has extended into a misinformed critique of Derridean architectural theorists, who are taken to task for privileging architectural writing over architectural practice. An attentive reading of Derrida will demonstrate the folly of such assumptions: simply to reverse the privileging flow, to privilege the previously inferior term over the previously superior term, is to remain within the same system of privileging. Writing, then, can reveal this, but comes with its own pitfalls of logocentric construction. And this revelation upon revelation, emerging from reflexive critique—the thing at hand always throwing itself into question—constitutes the lesson of Derrida. Privileging, an ultimately static operation, gives way to oscillating (or shuttling), an operation that itself shuttles between stasis and flow.

In the translator's preface to *Of Grammatology,* Gayatri Spivak notes this oscillation as a kind of topological move (slipping into one another), in approaching the relation of writing as conventionally construed (a kind of transparent medium through which speech [presence] expresses itself) to "writing" as a repressed structure that both precedes and organizes speech and as the instrument for the expression of its own repressions:

> The repression of writing in the narrow sense is a pervasive symptom of centrism. . . . The usual notion of writing in the narrow sense does contain the elements of the structure of writing in general: the absence of the "author" and of the "subject-matter," interpretability, the deployment of a space and a time that is not "its own." We "recognize" all this in writing in the narrow sense and "repress" it; this allows us to ignore that everything else is also inhabited by the structure of writing in general, that "the thing itself always escapes." . . . Derrida's choice of the words "writing" or "arche-writing" is thus not fortuitous. Indeed, as Derrida repeatedly points out in the section on Lévi-Strauss, no rigorous distinction between writing in the narrow and the general senses can be made. One slips into the other, putting the distinction under erasure. Writing has had the negative privilege of being the scapegoat whose exclusion represents the definition of the metaphysical enclosure. (lxix) [4]

Weaving itself (a shuttling operation) is figured in its origins by expressions of repressions. Weaving is the invention and activity of the inferior term of the male-female pair; it is also a surrogate of speech. In providing an explanation for the anomaly of women making a contribution to culture, Sigmund Freud suggested that they originated the art of weaving by plaiting their pubic hair in order to mask the absence of the penis and what the penis represents in society: the phallus and the power to prescribe and inscribe lines of legitimacy. Weaving for Freud therefore becomes a silent substitute for the power of speech. But, as Ann Bergren has demonstrated, there is a paradox (a shuttling) at work in the text of weaving:

> Greek culture inherits from Indo-European a metaphor by which poets and prophets define themselves as "weaving" or "sewing" words. . . . They call their product, in effect, a "metaphorical web." But which, then, is the original and which the metaphorical process? Is weaving a figurative speech or is poetry a figurative web? The question cannot be decided. Weaving as the sign-making activity of women is both literal and metaphorical, both original and derived. It is, like the Muses' speech, ambiguously true speech and an imitation of true speech.
>
> The myth of Tereus, Procne and Philomela provides a good example. It testifies to the regular limitation of women to tacit weaving, while exposing the magical power of a silent web to speak. When Tereus, the husband of Procne, rapes her sister Philomela, he cuts out the woman's tongue to keep her silent, but Philomela, according to Apollodorus (3.14.8), *huphenasa en peploi grammata* "wove pictures/writing (*grammata* can mean either) in a robe" which she sent to her sister. Philomela's trick reflects *the "trickiness" of weaving, its uncanny ability to make meaning out of inarticulate matter, to make silent material speak* [emphasis mine]. In this way, women's weaving is, as *grammata* implies, a "writing" or graphic art, a silent, material representation of audible, immaterial speech. ("Language and the Female," 71–73)

The woven thing, then, is more than a mere pathetic substitute for a lack. It bears the ability to enable a resurfacing of something that has lain hidden, that has been repressed. A text is more than writing in the narrow sense, much more than a transparent medium through which speech or truth is expressed. The word *grammata* is a significant joint, as it connects both back to Derrida and grammatology and over into another textual field generative of this work: the work of Walter Benjamin on allegory.

Benjamin's 1928 treatise on allegory, *Ursprung des deutschen Trauerspiels* (*The Origin of German Tragic Drama*), a work contemporaneous to *Finnegans Wake,*[5] was conceived as a tissue (*histos*) of quotations whose logic derived from an emblematic armature (making the treatise itself allegorical, an example of that which it addresses). One of the predominant characteristics of Benjamin's construction of allegory is a slippage of the boundary between visual and verbal criteria. The hieroglyph, a form of picture writing, is the instrument he uses to demonstrate and elucidate his notion of allegory. (See my chapter 1, "Allegory and the Possibility of Architecture.") Hieroglyphic writing has come down to us preserved as engravings upon stone tablets, obelisks, or sarcophagi, which ties it to cutting and incising in its methods and to three-dimensional objects in its media,[6] as well as in its cryptlike character (the voids in the stone that describe the "pictures" are themselves spatial). Modern scholars have imbued hieroglyphic writing with a quality of secretiveness that is due to its displacement in time of translatability and their attendant theories concerning its probable use only by certain initiated persons authorized to learn its secrets. Hieroglyphic writing is then cryptic as well as cryptlike, in the sense that it consists of voids carved into solid material. Hieroglyphic writing as thus construed becomes an instrument of communicating ideas that must be kept secret from some, a writing of that which cannot be spoken. In these senses, it is tied to weaving and poetry and *grammata*. In *The Narrative of Arthur Gordon Pym*, Edgar Allan Poe provides a connection among spatiality, writing, and secretiveness in the cryptic caves discovered and described by the presumed narrator.

In its ambiguous emblematicity of "crypt," and its ambiguous position between picture and writing, the hieroglyph suggests a writing that is other than transparent, a writing that is illegible in the conventional sense, a writing in which repressions surface. This "writing" might be termed *(s)crypt*. It is the writing of Joyce and the writing (etching) of Piranesi, which give themselves up to other readings. At points this writing appears in the form of—merges with—conventional writing. In *Finnegans Wake,* this sort of intersection takes the shape, for example, of the letter "T," which both occupies proper places in the proper sequencing of letters of words and forms patterns (mosaiclike) in the text, suggesting in a third valence the post and beam of architectural trabeation, and in a fourth and fifth the watery connection of tea and micturition (tee-tee) as they are underlaid by the feminine signifier (water, the river) in the symbolic order of the text itself. In this construction, the intersection frequently takes the form of the letter "X," which signifies the chiasmic armature itself of this kind of ambiguity, as well as referring to its markings in the writings of Derrida (the *chiasmus*, the *pharmakon*, the *supplément, différance*), in addition to playing in the space between this text and the letter's conventional significations. A noteworthy chiasmus marked by the letter "X," and one that the present work foregrounds, is that of theory and practice. This may be seen not only as an intersection of two different "lines" but also (and importantly) as a mirrored image, two sides of the same thing. By swerving out of the conventional theoretical treatise both in form (the present text is situated ambiguously between a conventional scholarly work and an architectonic construction) and in methodology (it operates in the spaces among poststructuralism, Marxism, and feminism, all of which have points of attachment to the logocentric bonds of conventional scholarly research while remaining critical of such research), the text itself occupies this critical-cryptic chiasmic space.

The Construction of *Finnegans Wake*

On more than one occasion, James Joyce referred to himself as an architect. *Finnegans Wake* is a monumental construction, a quasi three-dimensional text, and in its interwoven and colliding geometries, its incorporation of familiar, old materials and entities and fragments, its various connections, and its ambiguous signification it contains an intricate architectonic that reinforces its identity with the city. It is an allegorical work, a multi-layered palimpsest, bits and pieces of previous and succeeding texts read through other texts.

At issue is the question of how *Finnegans Wake* might inform an architecture that is not theory-bound, or an architecture that is about displaying the fallacies of its theories. The ways in which Joyce's text divorces itself from the literary tradition are useful here.

The story, or narrative, of the book does not unroll along a line of time. Its units of narrative are assembled in space—in the space of the text. Thus the text pushes at a privileging of spatiality over temporality. (It is important to remember that post-Enlightenment Western architecture and architectural theory are founded in modes of thinking that are predominantly linear and rational—temporal, not spatial—regardless of the prevalence of the notion that architecture is a discourse on spatiality.) This foregrounding of spatiality allows Joyce's text to become peculiarly resonant with the poststructuralist exploration of the spaces of writing.

The narrative assemblage of bits and pieces that is *Finnegans Wake* forces an abandonment of the idea of reader as a passive receptor. The reader must engage, work on, rewrite this text. The reader must be a writer. She or he must be the kind of reader described by Julia Kristeva in *Semiotike*:

> For the Ancients the verb "to read" had a meaning that is worth recalling and bringing out with a view to an understanding of literary practice. "To read" was also "to pick up," "to pluck," "to keep a watch on," "to recognize traces," "to take," "to steal." "To read" thus denotes an aggressive participation, an active appropriation of the other. "To write" would be "to read" become production, industry: writing-reading, paragrammatic activity, would be the aspiration towards a total aggressiveness and participation. (181)

This reader-writer is a producer, an appropriator, a maker, an assembler. This is also the kind of writer about whom Roland Barthes writes in an essay on Michel Butor's *Mobile*: "Michel Butor has conceived his novels as a single structural investigation whose principle might be this: it is by *tying* fragments of events together that meaning is generated, it is by tirelessly transforming these events into functions that the structure is erected: the writer (poet, novelist, chronicler) *sees* the meaning of the inert units in front of him only by *relating* them" (*Critical Essays*, 182–183). Michel Butor, *Mobile*:

> Four o'clock in GREENEVILLE. My husband is sleeping beside me. Fairy Cave. TROY, county seat of Lincoln County. He doesn't know my dreams. Crystal Caverns, Marvel Cave. TROY. A shudder in the grass. Turns. TROY. Shudder in all these beds. Tracery. TROY. A shudder on the lake water. Loops. TROY, PA. On the river water. Meanders. TROY, N.Y. A shudder from the sea. Charms. At night right angles begin vibrating. The hissing of serpents echoing from square to square. (147–148)

Here is also an association with cinematic montage.[7] In montage, the sense of temporal discontinuity created by the technique is superseded by the viewer-created synthesis of meaning among relations of images.

David Hayman writes: "Tales reveal their analogical freight before they spill their 'action.' Visual and verbal effects vie for our attention." And the reader processes the language, "becomes the text without losing himself as he reads" (*Wake of the* Wake, 7).

In *Finnegans Wake* Joyce manipulates the material—the ink marks on the page that become signifiers—in ways that allow it to exist at the borders between convention or rationality and madness. Signifiers do not signify in a linear or hierarchical fashion but in multiple directions: they slide, they move, suggesting a space created by the signifier as it indicates the directions of its own movement through fields of knowledge. The material exhibits similarity on multiple levels to Freudian mechanisms of signification (condensation and displacement) in dreams.

The material is manipulated through strategies of:

Deformation
  Splitting
  Multiplication
Repetition
  Motifs
  Numbers
  Geometrical configurations (Euclidean and Non-Euclidean)
Collision
  Portmanteau words (two or more words that "collide" to form one)
Ambiguity
  Sliding signifiers
  Portmanteau words
  A dominant presence of hermaphroditic emblems
Necessity to use extra-visual senses to decipher
  Blurring of distinctions between visual and verbal
  Homophonies
Superimposition
  Of Structures
  Of disseminated material
  Of semantic content (ambiguity)
Fragmentation
Thematic weaving and layering
  "Phenomenal Transparency"
Absence of hierarchies

Plays of resemblances

Presence of syntactic armatures

Residues of process left in the object

Excess

Reflexivity

Self-allegorizing

It is important to bear in mind that reflexivity of strategy goes on in the text as well, such that each residual of a strategic move is subject to manipulation by any of the others. The moves are thus potentially infinitely generative.

Spatial metaphors are often used in writing about *Finnegans Wake*. This does not suggest an absence of chronological structures, however. The text is less a narrative to be apprehended than an object to be entered, less narrated than constructed. Within its construction are many voices telling, but even so, the tales being told have less presence than the material being manipulated in the telling.

It is made from parts found or stolen, appropriated, plagiarized; things then twisted, deformed, manipulated so as to join readily to their neighbors. It concerns neighbors and spatial relations, not sequences of events and causes and effects. It is, in a sense, like Gilles Deleuze and Félix Guattari's description of the construction that vandals stealing from the museum make with the stolen bits. It should be noted, however, that this comparison would not sit well with the pertinent text (*Franz Kafka: Towards a Minor Literature*), in which Deleuze and Guattari pose Joyce as differing from Kafka in reterritorializing rather than deterritorializing. Joyce works in richness, Kafka in poverty.

In *Finnegans Wake*, conventional syntax is suppressed. In places, it nearly fades away altogether. The identities between units or words are based not so much on a grammatical system as on the creation of systems in which layers of meaning lie waiting for discovery. It therefore parallels architecture, with its spare, rudimentary syntactical element (capital on top of column, arches repeat from springpoints),[8] and, as a model, suggests a backgrounding of syntax.

It is politically subversive. Joyce declared himself to be both anti-classical and antiromantic (see Hart, *Structure and Motif in* Finnegans Wake). Philippe Sollers writes of this analysis of "2000 years of manwomankind":

Finnegans Wake teems with "answers," but these answers are not of a scientific order; they come from a knowledge that will never present itself as systematic, any more than as definitively centered or serious. This is why it is a matter of the most forceful act ever accomplished against political paranoia and the overhanging weight of its deadening discourse, outside of all humor. Let me stress then that *Finnegans Wake* is the most formidably antifascist book produced between the two wars. ("Joyce & Co.," *Wake of the* Wake, 108–109)[9]

With *Finnegans Wake,* Joyce made an enormous challenge to the idea that language is simply an instrument for mirroring reality. In this text, language is not reproduction, but production. It is not about "What does it mean?" but "How does it work?"[10] It is an exploration of the nature of structure. The question is both the form and the content of the work (see Norris, *Decentered Universe*).

The question both embraces and goes beyond Ferdinand de Saussure's location of significance in relations and structures rather than in transparent contents of elements. This embrace of the arbitrary nature of the linguistic sign is "fundamental" to *Finnegans Wake*. (So is a corresponding focus on synchronic relations in language.) But the "meaning" generated by those relations and structures rarely approaches something unified or even gathered. It is scattered, dispersed, disseminated. As in Poe's story "The Purloined Letter," all the information is present.[11] The (localized) "meanings" we are seduced into seeking are red herrings, in schools. By going beyond Saussure, beyond seeking friction-generated (relation-generated) "meaning," we come back to seeing simply the correspondences themselves. In *Finnegans Wake,* "How does it work?" *is* "What does it mean?"

The French critic Hélène Cixous writes of the work: "The linear construction of the [ordinary sentence] is burst asunder and replaced by a kind of verbal galaxy" (*Exile of James Joyce,* 606). She then lays out an argument that suggests the blurring of visual and verbal categories in allegory, implying that the allegorizing of James Joyce operates on a smaller scale as well as on the more obvious large one:

> At a certain level of prose and of the artist's sensibility, the word and the perceptible appearance of the thing resuscitate similar visions, as though the word itself were an object which one encountered and turned into epiphany. . . . Often a chain-reaction

is set up, and a word calls up a vision that, as it fades, calls up further words to mark its passage. Joyce or the artist, because he is aware of this process, requires language more and more to serve as his meeting-place with reality; he is constantly on the watch for the word or fact which he feels he needs. (606)

Language here is construed not as a mirror but as a constellation of points of exchange, a kind of switching mechanism of potential transformations.

At this point, the language of *Finnegans Wake* is revealed as a generative paradigm of deconstructive criticism. Vincent Leitch writes that *Finnegans Wake* is a text "where licentious dissemination creates a different order of reading" (*Deconstructive Criticism*, 202). *Finnegans Wake* is an obsessive misreading. Joyce blurs distinctions among reading and raiding and writing, between beginnings and endings, between the visual and the verbal, and demonstrates the procrustean absurdity of bipolar logic:

> The prouts who will invent a writing there ultimately is the poeta, still more learned, who discovered the raiding there originally. That's the point of eschatology our book of kills reaches for now in soandso many counterpoint words. What can't be coded can be decorded if an ear aye sieze what no eye ere grieved for. Now, the doctrine obtains, we have occasioning cause causing effects and affects occasionally recausing altereffects. (*FW*, 482.31–483.01)

A Guided Tour of the Construction (What It Is and How to Read It)

This book (following the present section) consists of an introduction that addresses the subject of allegory and architecture while mapping a reading of Walter Benjamin's *Origin of German Tragic Drama* (*Ursprung des deutsches Trauerspiels*), in order to theorize the three-plus-one constructions that follow. The first three constructions are assemblages of texts upon the armatures of three drawings or sets of drawings of Piranesi. They are *Finnegans Wake*-derived constructions in the sense that they involve the strategic operations of making discussed above, and they are also informed by readings of contemporary criticism. Like the chapters of *Finnegans Wake*, they are structured as well upon a simple Euclidean geometry: the Euclidean device for producing an equilateral triangle known as the *vesica piscis,* an emblematic diagram featured in *Finnegans Wake.* The first and third constructions are assembled upon circular armatures that intersect in various ways, the middle construction upon the superimposition of the circles and the triangle. The vesica piscis is an allegorical emblem of the present work that operates, as emblems do, on many levels.

The linear path from the first to the third construction will also reveal a mediated dialectic that is one of the themes of this work as well as a major theme of twentieth-century linguistic concern: that of the spoken and the written language. The first construction (*Campo Marzio*) relies upon its writtenness and is constructed as an essay that pushes, in Benjaminian fashion, the limits of the essay form. The third construction (*Carceri*) demands to be read aloud as the reader reads, for many of its connections, both at the macro and micro levels, depend upon homophonies (much as does much of *Finnegans Wake*). The middle construction (*Collegio*) lies between these extremes, as a place of blurring, somewhere between the essay and the nursery rhyme—possibly within the realm of an architecture.

The construction that follows the three, and perhaps belongs in their set (by being a kind of underlayment to the three) and perhaps does not, both adheres to and explodes the bounds of logocentric trinitarian symmetry. It is a re-turn to Benjamin, both modelled after and appropriating fragments of his *Passagen-Werk.* It is entitled "Un Chateau des cartes," simultaneously a House of Cards and a Cartesian House. The vesica piscis again appears, emblematizing the ambiguity of building and text by allowing for an oscillation among the architectural construction of John Soane, the textual construction of James Joyce, and the theoretical construction of Walter Benjamin. This house, as in the case of many constructions, is haunted by a ghost and contains secrets in its closets. It is an allegory of that which this text theorizes and is a residual of a particular kind of practice.

There is no "conclusion" to this text. At the point of its page with the highest number, the text is either brought full circle or to the point of beginning another circle (another reading). The *Syllapsies* ("graspings") serves as a switching mechanism for two alternate, nonlinear readings. One reading begins in the Syllapsies and maps the territory of each motif (appearing throughout the book as bracketed words in capital letters) across the construction. The other operates from the linear text, but takes off to the

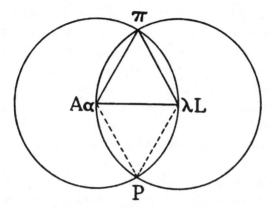

Vesica Piscis

Syllapsies by means of the marked motifs, at which point it can return to the text at many possible points (anywhere else the motif appears). This reading imitates the construction of *le jeu de l'oie* (the game of goose), a game that is both a subject and a structure here.

In the reading, the object is always turning around on itself. There are multiple points where it involutes, Klein worm–like, and allows wormy or moley routes that let other parts be drawn through. It is in this sense a three-dimensional map of "systems" of ideas, documents, and configuring diagrams represented as black marks upon a page. It is not exactly a writing as "writing" is conventionally constituted, nor is it exactly a "drawing" as such. It oscillates between writing and drawing, operating in the spaces between. The conventional allegorical painting, which requires the reading and viewing operator-cum-interpreter to engage the space between the linguistic and the graphic, is a simple model of this: that "space between" must be explored, or built within, in order to construe the relations between the two. The present text is such a construction. Thus, it is not a treatise that proposes a theory of architecture and text, but a paratheoretical construction of architecture and text. It relies upon *transformative* operations. In *Positions* Jacques Derrida writes:

> Within the limits of its possibility, or its *apparent* possibility, translation practices the difference between signified and signifier. But, if this difference is never pure, translation is even less so, and a notion of *transformation* must be substituted for the notion of translation: a regulated transformation of one language by another, of one text by another. We shall not have and never have had to deal with some "transfer" of pure signifieds that the signifying instrument—or "vehicle"—would leave virgin and intact, from one language to another, or within one and the same language. (trans. Spivak in preface to Derrida, *Grammatology*, lxxxvii)

To which Gayatri Spivak responds: " 'From one language to another, or within one and the same language.' Translation is a version of the intertextuality that comes to bear also within the 'same' language" (preface to Derrida, *Grammatology*, lxxxvii). The language of *Finnegans Wake* is to the point here. It is the same and not the same language (on both sides of the language fence—architectural and linguistic).[12]

The language of *Finnegans Wake* is always oscillating and trans-forming. The signified-signifier associations are under constant relocation, offering continuous slippage and dissemination into multiple possibilities of meaning. There is an aspect of simultaneity of chronological and achrono-logical structures. This is not to suggest frozen time (nor "frozen music"), a notion that merely leaves us still with a kind of chicken or egg choice. It is the simultaneity that must be grasped.[13]

An exploration of the architectonics of *Finnegans Wake* involves operations upon the text that can be described as digging, peeling away, cut-ting, and dissecting, operations that in revealing the structures of the text simultaneously reveal processes of making in the text. The text is architec-tonic and is as well intensely allegorical. It is a model that might underlie a theory of architecture analogous to Paul Ricoeur's historiographical con-struction in the gap between narrative understanding and historical explana-tion, a construction that involves the superimposition of chronological and achronological structures (see *Time and Narrative*, volume 1).

The superimposition of the chronological and the achronologi-cal—form and process, perhaps—is crucial to the concept of allegory, the "epitome of counter-narrative," as Craig Owens puts it (see "Allegorical Impulse"), which nevertheless references temporality. In mapping out the schema of what an allegorical architecture might be, we can borrow almost wholesale Walter Benjamin's constellation of terms circumscribing allegory: countering classicism, born of a "strange combination of nature and history," hieroglyphic (existing between the visual and the verbal), a simultaneous elevation and devaluation of the profane world, both convention and expres-sion, form and technique, analogous to the ruin, palimpsestic, constructed of fragments, subject to simultaneous "dispersal" and "collectedness," a "pro-fusion of emblems . . . grouped around [a] figural centre" (*Origin*, 167, 188).

By sifting through the history of architecture, examples of such an architecture can be found: the work of Francesco Borromini, of Giambattista Piranesi, the house-museum of John Soane, and Carlo Scarpa's Castelvec-chio renovation, among others. (The history of allegorical architecture is itself allegorical.) The pastiche of postmodern architecture was only a feeble allegorical gesture. With its accompanying rhetoric about figure and sym-bol, it was not allegorical in theory. A more potent infusion of the allegori-cal impulse into contemporary architecture could move architecture away from its reactionary position in culture, and, more immediately, away from issues of style-qua-image (such as "postmodernism" and "deconstructivism") altogether.

But what happens to the building in this constellation of ideas? The status of the building itself as it is multiply (and simultaneously) positioned within its architectural history and the history of architecture and the theories of history is a case in point.[14] The building is the object of the history of architecture, but it is a slippery kind of object with respect to theories of history. The building is a document of something that happened. It is a document of great transparency (translatability), because it is the concretization of what happened (mediated by the historian—the "agent," in historical terms, of the document is absent). Simultaneously it is a document of extreme opacity because of its use as a functional object over time (and its consequent physical functional change over time); because of its consumption-appropriation over time—the building serves as a model for other buildings; and, the nature of this consumption being historically more appropriative than allusive, because of a difficulty in "reading" it as a single document. (The Tempietto of Bramante is an example.)

The building is almost what actually happened. It is not only document; it is event itself. It can be construed as meeting the criteria of Paul Ricoeur in *Time and Narrative* for eventhood. There is, however, an area in which it displays its slipperiness again—that is, with respect to Ricoeur's first epistemological criterion, that an event is an unrepeatable singularity. There is a sense in which the building is repeatable—the octastyle peripteral Greek temple, for example, can be repeated, or even the Parthenon. On the other hand, the Parthenon on the Acropolis at Athens is a singular "event." But, then again, because it undergoes repetition of itself in its restoration, it is not. So, the Parthenon that was constructed by Ictinos and Callicrates on the Acropolis at Athens in the reign of Pericles is the singular event. But now we have gone beyond the building: we have connected it to time and the history of actions. There is an oscillation, or a simultaneity, of the status of a building with regard to history: it is both an object that is repeatable, or lends itself toward repetition, and an object that exists in a complex network of actions.

The existence of the building is, then, textual, and depends upon a mental construct of space and time that is not bipolar, not even dialectical.

Architecture in this sense (and architectural theory) is, to a degree, "always already" allegorical in the Benjaminian sense. That is, architecture contains the instrument for radical critical operations upon itself within itself. "The strategy of criticism is located in the object of criticism" (Serres, *Hermes*, 38).

The overarching strategy of this book is a mapping of the interwoven complexes of systematicity punctuated by constellations of joints that constitute architecture itself. As he or she approaches my construction, the reader should carry a sense of the building as an object of mind-boggling ideational intricacy, connected to history and culture so as to form a knotty textuality that mimes a building's physical complexity.

Allegory
and the
Possibility
of
Architecture

It is well known that the potato is a root vegetable that grows in stony soil and has Irish affiliations. The potato, which grows in the dark, sports grotesque protuberances known as eyes. When digging for these tubers, one must sift through many [STONE]s before finding all the potatoes contained within the volume of soil at hand. There are seven potatoes in the children's rhyme and there are seven potatoes in this stony text. It may take some digging to find them.

One Potato

Humpty Dumpty sat on a wall
Humpty Dumpty had a great fall
All the king's horses and all the king's men
Couldn't put Humpty Dumpty and his bleeding, seeping,
    exuding, leaking, dribbling, trickling, oozing, streaming,

flowing, discharging, runny, riveting, emissive self
together again.

P.S. Had he not fallen among stones, this story might have been
different.

Before we come into the world, we are beings in motion, blind projects in the dark, bodies tossed and rolled, rocked, on the move. Once we come in, assaulted by the light, rocking makes us feel at home. We are nomads born, haptic creatures, and we spend our lives forgetting it. Architecture is the evidence of this denial. It stands between the unrepresentable and us. Our existential projects are the denial of death by the denial of bodies, immortalizing by the veiling of the mortal. We pile up stones feverishly in an attempt to reproduce the container, the vessel, the thing, producing the image at the expense of the voluptuous. We, like Sisyphus, never reach the goal because the impossibility of so doing is programmed into the rules of the game.

Two Potato

I have a bone to pick—or chomp on—with the recent "alliance" of architecture with the discourses of deterritorialization and dissemination that all comes out as style. "What does it look like?" is not the same question as "How does it work?" or "What is the itinerary?" or "What constitutes the assemblage?" But perhaps the bone I think I am biting is my own tail.[1] Perhaps Mark Wigley has played a vague and duplicitous game, operating on a razor's edge, making deconstruction so ridiculous a proposition that, now happily and easily consumed as having something to do with an architectural "look" (as in "I don't know how to define it, but I know it when I see it"), the margins have been cleared.[2] In the realm of the possibility of this "perhaps," even the grosse pierre has been rolled aside, leaving a gaping dark hole. The work can now begin. Again.

Perhaps: David pitched a well-aimed pebble and hit Goliath where it hurts (in the eye). Folks who live in glass houses should beware of inviting in boys who talk softly but carry big slingshots.

Three Potato

Sometimes pebbles seem simply to be underfoot, as in the following morsel from Roger Kimball, writing for the *New Criterion* in June 1988. The piece is called "The Death and Resurrection of Postmodern Architecture," and it is about rolling away the same big rock: "Immersed in Mr. Eisenman's chatter, one easily forgets that architecture is essentially about building habitable buildings, buildings that we live in and work in, play and worship in, not buildings that we struggle to decode" (26).

Let us crack open a few of these stones. "Immersed": we are under water, perhaps in hot water, perhaps we are drowning, in chatter. (To chatter is to verbalize whatever comes to mind, without restraint or order [BABEL].) Heterosexual white adult males Do Not Chatter. Who chatters? Magpies, women, children, black mammies and jovial Uncle Toms in the movies, flamboyant gay males. Peter Eisenman has been hit where it hurts; with a word, his position in the power structure has been challenged. Architecture is here a simple, unified discipline with its own pure essence: building habitable buildings. The Being (essence) of architecture is building buildings in which we dwell. A familiar model. But Kimball fails to mention the thinking part of architectural *Dasein,* putting it by implication over in another category, that of "struggling to decode." To decode presumes a prior encoding, which is implied here as an additional facet of *not essentially architecture.* And this *not* draws the line and ties it at both ends. With this *not,* Kimball has laid the cards of positivism on the table. The duality *not architecture/architecture* can be mapped as follows:

Eisenman	*architecture*
chatter	essence
drowning	building and dwelling
struggling	living/working/playing
decoding	worshiping

Clearly, Eisenman is not on the side of architecture.

Four

Architecture stands. *Stat.* "Fidem meam obligo vexillo civitatium Americae Federatarum, et rei publicae pro qua stat. Uni natione, deo ducendi, non dividendae, cum libertate iustitiaque omnibus." [3] Architecture stands and stands for. Like a flag or symbol, a sign. *Pro qua stat? Pro statu quo.* Architecture is the supplement of—it both stands in for and is in excess of—the State, the *civitas, pro qua stat.* The power of architecture rests in its potential to stand up and in for the powerful, the potentate, which stands under and in for the Omnipotent. When the nation under God bleeds out of its boundaries and finds itself in a state of global multinational capitalism, the questions "Who are all?" and "What are liberty and justice?" become difficult, slippery. When that for which architecture stands becomes slippery and difficult, it stands to reason that architecture becomes slippery and difficult.

The sorceress-hysterics of Hélène Cixous appear as repressed-other makers in Monique Wittig's *Les Guérillères.* In this fictional world, the women use the tools of patriarchal material culture to make assemblages that work against it. They make a [MINOR ARCHITECTURE]: they collect the tools of capitalist culture—mass production machinery of all sorts, washing machines, vacuum cleaners, and stoves—and make of them a great allegorical dumping ground, a petrified landscape, which they set on fire.

> Then, starting to dance around it, they clap their hands, they shout obscene phrases, they cut their hair or let it down. When the fire has burnt down, when they are sated with setting off explosions, they collect the debris, the objects that are not consumed, those that have not melted down, those that have not disintegrated. They cover them with blue green red paint to reassemble them in grotesque grandiose abracadabrant compositions to which they give names. (93)

These are Towers of [BABEL], chatterers' architecture, the [HATCHERY], an architecture of the carnivalesque that has egressed from the sanctioned and bounded midway.[4] The amusement park or funhouse is the reification and topos of (still) authoritatively controlled desire. Desire here is filtered through an assemblage of safety valves. Power and ideology are as present as they are in the Pentagon, or perhaps more to the point, as they are in the Penthouse, where desire is reconstituted as will to power and served up as sexuality. (In this sense, the pet is better clothed than the emperor.) What is pent up in the Penthouse or the funhouse is the desire of the other, which apparently is not satisfied (as the barkers in the midway or the caption writers would have us believe) by being petrified, objectified.

The ejaculations of the other, when they come, are not easily wiped away. They can be messy and ugly, hysterical constructions, "grotesque grandiose abracadabrant compositions," circulating partial objects. Dark, polysemous, and out of control, like a dreamy fall.

For the other, the Penthouse, the fun house, and the prison [HOUSE] [5] bear a remarkable similarity: they are orderly stacks of "mill and stumpling [STONE]s." And, as Nietzsche reminds us, we will more easily break a leg in our stumblings than one of these stones. It is a losing battle to attempt to tear down or replace these solid constructions. We must rather build "unsafe buildings" in their shadows.

> Inasmuch as [history] is a criticism of signifying practices, it will have to "shift the stones" by shifting around its own stones. Criticism speaks only if the doubt with which it attacks the real turns back on itself as well. Operating on its own constructions, history makes an incision with a scalpel in a body whose scars do not disappear; but at the same time, unhealed scars already mar the compactness of historical constructions, rendering them problematic and preventing them from presenting themselves as "truth." . . . The certainties that history presents should . . . be read as *expressions of repressions*. They are nothing but defenses or barriers that hide the reality of historical writing. They incorporate uncertainty: "true history" is not that which cloaks itself in indisputable "philological proofs," but that which recognizes its own arbitrariness, which recognizes itself as an "unsafe building." (Tafuri, *Sphere and Labyrinth*, 12)

An unsafe construction, then, not only questions its object of criticism, but always throws itself into crisis as well. The work is always in progress. It is generative. It is never complete, never completely clear.

> She had been working on it for fifteen years, carrying about with her a shapeless bag of dingy, threadbare brocade containing odds and ends of colored fabric in all possible shapes. She could never bring herself to trim them to any pattern; so she shifted and fitted and mused and fitted and shifted them like pieces of a patient puzzle-picture, trying to fit them to a pattern or create a pattern about them without using her scissors, smoothing her colored scraps with flaccid, putty-colored fingers, shifting and

shifting them. From the bosom of her dress the needle Narcissa had threaded for her dangled its spidery skein [PATCHWORK]. (Faulkner, *Sartoris*, 151–152)

Architecture is the material expression that stands for (*stat*) ideology. It also stands in the metaphor of hierarchical and structural thinking (gravity, Cartesian logic). It is tautological (Joyce's "tootoological"), it is incised, and in this sense Eisenman is right: "Architecture will always look like architecture" ("Architecture as a Second Language," 73). But the "looks like" must be called into question.

An architecture of desire—a [MINOR ARCHITECTURE]—will operate in the interstices of this architecture. Not opposed to, not separate from, but upon/within/among: barnacles, bastard constructions (*une bâtarde architecture*) tattoos (ornament, embellishment). An other writing upon the body of architecture. Architecture becomes the ground, or stone, on which its [MAPPING] is inscribed—on which its processes bleed. Kafka.

Five Potato

Allos agoreuein: "The other speaks in public," in the *agora*. For the other, as for Walter Benjamin—reject, outcast, melancholic, who met his end among pure, finely cut, white, proper stones—the line between the political and the personal is utterly imaginary. The contest between the libidinal and the political, desire and ideology, is no contest.

As Craig Owens has pointed out, Walter Benjamin's theory of allegory "defies summary" (see "Allegorical Impulse"). Benjamin's text is a [PATCHWORK] of fragments and seams, stitched both horizontally across each layer of pieces and vertically through the layers to hold the thing together. Because Benjamin's treatise on allegory and *Trauerspiel* is itself allegorical, it is not approachable by summation (which would merely be a recitation of the text at best). It is, however, appropriate to plot an itinerary through this text, and by so doing, to map it (misread it).

Benjamin's treatise is an "exasperated articulation of a theme [allegory] originally taken as absolute," a critical experimentalism of Tafuri's type "E," the classification of "Piranesi's *Iconographia* Campi Martii, of many 'critical restorations' by Albini and Scarpa, of Kahn's last work" (Tafuri, *Theories and History*, 111). And, one might add, of James Joyce's *Finnegans*

Wake (an "exasperated articulation" of the "nightmare from which I am trying to awake").

Let us begin with the word *emblem*. "In the baroque, especially, the allegorical personification can be seen to give way in favour of the emblems, which mostly offer themselves to view in desolate, sorrowful dispersal" (Benjamin, *Origin*, 186). An emblem (in German, *Sinnbild*, which carries a perverse homophonous similarity to *symbol*, and an even more appropriately perverse homophonous similarity to *sin-build*, suggesting a connection to illicit building) is an image that serves as a decoding apparatus for an allegory. Emblems, which "mostly offer themselves to view in desolate, sorrowful dispersal" (186), are themselves kinds of maps of the complex, fragmented, hieroglyphic mode of allegory that Benjamin finds in baroque tragic drama (and also well-seeded in sections of early modernism: in Baudelaire, for example). In their dispersal, the emblems that serve as switching mechanisms of Benjaminian allegory differ radically from the personifications of conventional allegory, which possess simple, causal relations between figure and meaning. Benjamin cites Johann Joachim Winckelmann's *Versuch einer Allegorie besonders für die Kunst:* "The best and most perfect allegory of one or of several concepts is comprised of one single figure, or should be thought of as such." And Friedrich Creuzer: "The German emblem . . . is quite lacking in that dignity and substance. It ought therefore . . . to remain confined to the lower sphere, and be completely excluded from symbolic tests" (*Origin*, 186).

Here, Benjamin is setting up an opposition between emblem and symbol (or the allegorical and the symbolic). What he accomplishes is a decisive cleavage between types of allegory. Both involve "convention and expression," but what I shall call conventional allegory, as opposed to Benjaminian allegory, "is not convention of expression [which points in the direction of allegory's connection to writing], but expression of convention [and] expression of authority, which is secret in accordance with the dignity of its origin, but public in accordance with the extent of its validity" (*Origin*, 175).

A return to *emblem* will allow us access to this cleavage, this place between, this perhaps abysmal split. The Latin word *emblema* means "inlaid work," like mosaic (made of bits of stone) or like certain ("primitive") forms of jewelry. ("Metalworking was the 'barbarian,' or nomad, art par excellence": Deleuze and Guattari, *Thousand Plateaus*, 401.) The Latin word emerged from the Greek *emballein,* which means "to throw in."[6] The act of making of a pot or jug or [VESSEL] is called throwing. Twisting fibers into thread, which is then wound about the *rochetto,* a shuttling projectile [ROCKET] used to make textiles, is also called throwing. Throwing is casting, as in casting a fishing line (which describes a trajectory) or casting a shadow (which describes a projection). To throw up is to evacuate the stomach of contents. When accomplished hurriedly, this is called projectile vomiting. To throw up is also to erect a construction hurriedly. If we trace a trajectory back through *throw* to the Latin, we encounter the verb *iaceo,* "I throw," whose past participle (*iactum*) is embedded in the object, the project, and the trajectory, as well as in rejection, abjection, and injection. And ejaculate.

A throw is also a radius described by a crank or cam in a machine. Which returns us to Benjamin and the distinction between symbol and allegory.[7] For Benjamin, the "genuine" concept of the symbol comes from theology, a paradoxical concept of "the unity of the material and the transcendental object." He castigates the nineteenth-century romantic aestheticians for distorting the concept into a simplistic one that is dependent on an "indivisible unity of form and content." In such a construct, "the beautiful is supposed to merge with the divine in an unbroken whole," making a perfect, circular relation between what something looks like and what it is (between appearance and essence). Benjamin insists that the cornerstone of this nineteenth-century idea was laid in classicism. His lengthy description of the "harmonious inwardness" of the classical subject and the classical conception of the symbol is worth quoting verbatim:

> In classicism the tendency to the apotheosis of existence in the individual who is perfect, in more than an ethical sense, is clear enough. What is typically romantic is the placing of this perfect individual within a progression of events which is, it is true, infinite but is nevertheless redemptive, even sacred. But once the ethical subject has become absorbed in the individual, then no rigorism—not even Kantian rigorism—can save it and preserve its masculine profile. Its heart is lost in the beautiful soul. And the radius of action—no, only the radius of the culture—of the thus perfected beautiful individual is what describes the circle of the "symbolic." In contrast the baroque apotheosis is a dialectical

one. It is accomplished in the movement between extremes. In this eccentric and dialectic process the harmonious inwardness of classicism plays no role, for the reason that the immediate problems of the baroque, being politico-religious problems, did not so much affect the individual and his ethics as his religious community. . . . Simultaneously with its profane concept of the symbol, classicism develops its speculative counterpart, that of the allegorical. A genuine theory of allegory did not, it is true, arise at that time, nor had there been one previously. It is nevertheless legitimate to describe the new concept of the allegorical as speculative because it was in fact adapted so as to provide the dark background against which the bright world of the symbol might stand out. (*Origin,* 160–161)

The opposition of symbol and allegory involves the centered, bright unity of the one and the eccentric, dark assemblage of the other in a figure-ground relation. Allegory is the other. It exists outside, but somehow lies underneath, both classical and romantic discourses.

In a series of twists, Benjamin demonstrates the identity of the modern (he names Yeats) and the nineteenth-century (he quotes Goethe and Schopenhauer) attitudes toward the allegory-symbol relation, an identity whose template is the alignment of symbol with the expression of Idea and the alignment of allegory with the expression of content. He thus retrieves from Schopenhauer's pejorative remarks on allegory one of the dominant structural elements of his own argument. Schopenhauer (in *The World as Will and Representation*) equates the expression of concept with "the trifling amusement of carving a picture to serve at the same time as an inscription, as a hieroglyphic" (quoted in *Origin,* 162). Benjamin takes Schopenhauer's dismissal of allegory as merely a form of writing (picture writing) and says, Yes! This is an important aspect of allegory, this muddying of the distinction between word and image, between the verbal and the visual. And here he suggests what Stephen Melville later states, that "the allegorical impulse is one which would acknowledge explicitly the futility of trying to sort the 'mere' from the 'pure' [*la mère* from *le père, la mer* from *la pierre*], an impulse to embrace the [heteronomous and heterological]" ("Notes on the Reemergence of Allegory," 80).

Manfredo Tafuri suggests (although he does not write it) that, be-

cause architecture is such a complex structure, it is always already of an allegorical impulse; for when "symbolic signs" are introduced into architecture,
they acquire an "*ambiguous* character":

> In reality every work of architecture can be referred to several
> symbolic systems. The fact that in Borromini's S. Ivo the myth of
> Babel's Tower, the ascent to Truth and Knowledge, the divine anti-
> [BABEL], the Pentecostal space, the superimposed [conventional]
> allegories of Modesty and Knowledge (the emblematic bee and
> the Domus Sapientiae as the seven-pillared house) are fused with
> the passage from a space uncertain of its hierarchy (that of the
> lower level) to the unitary space of the dome, is not irrelevant to
> the formation of meanings specific to the spatial in-fill. (*Theories
> and History*, 198)

Tafuri's architectural symbol (particularly in the example of Borromini),
resembles closely Benjamin's allegorical sign:

> The symbol is, in fact, something that because of its nature rejects
> an univocal reading. Its meanings tend to escape and its character-
> istic is that of *revealing and hiding at the same time*. Otherwise,
> instead of a symbol we should speak of an "emblem." . . . It fol-
> lows, therefore, that the qualities of the [architectural] symbol
> are the same as those of the artistic "sign": ambiguous, disposed
> to accept different meanings, transparent and fixed within a pre-
> established code, and, at the same time, able to transgress the laws
> of that code. (198, emphasis mine)

In another essay in the same book, Tafuri reports that, with the
rise of allegory and symbolism in the seventeenth and eighteenth centuries,
"architecture realises the impossibility of finding its own reasons exclusively
in itself" (80–82). The presence of an "interlocutor" who "does not simply
receive the messages, but . . . is asked to complete them, even to change
their meaning while they are being deciphered," is necessary to what Sedl-
mayer called "*architecture that describes itself*" (the work of Brown, Kent,
Chambers, Soane, and Lequeu, among others; 82). In the assemblages of the
so-called picturesque landscape gardens (or of Soane's museum), architecture's status as absolute object approaches that of the ambiguous and the
relative, moving from the autonomous to the didactic (in the vague direc-

tion of what Eisenman, in "Architecture as a Second Language," terms a "dislocating text of architecture." Tafuri points out:

> As didactical instruments they are turned towards man, awakening his senses and injecting into them, immediately afterwards, a critical stimulus: Nature, by now not a reflection of the divine Idea but a structure shared by man, can merge with the history of the entire human species, showing that the rational course of civilization is natural, because it moves (Gian Battista Vico) from the realm of the senses to that of the intellect. . . . The Gothic, Chinese, Classical and eclectic pavilions inserted [*emballein*] in the texture of a "nature trained to be natural," are ambiguous objects. They allude to something other than themselves, losing their semantic autonomy. It is the same phenomenon that will move into *major* architecture. (*Theories and History*, 82)

There are several points of intensity here. One lies in the term *major architecture*. *Major* is not only used; it is italicized. Major architecture implies the presence of another architecture, which would be, by the logic of the implication, *minor architecture*. And into this category of [MINOR ARCHITECTURE], it follows, the "ambiguous objects" fall. Thus, through Tafuri, the construction *minor architecture*, which may contain within it "ambiguous objects," "dislocating text of architecture," allegory, and decipherability, may be tracked to the constellation of architectural constructions as they exist in oscillating difference to their context at Kew Gardens. Kew, here, becomes the ghost of the expanded field with which Rosalind Krauss tracks the allegorical impulse in contemporary art. This vaguely minor architecture is an assemblage of partial objects, a tesseraic text, a [PATCHWORK]. (The picture of the picturesque—what it looks like—is overshadowed by the complex of joints.) And it stands in difference to major architecture, instruments of reflection of the "divine cosmos," Tablets of Stone with the WORD OF GOD writ large.

A second generative collision is located in Tafuri's merging of interlocution and decipherment. At the point where the messages of *"l'architecture parlante"* are intercepted by an "interlocutor," speech shifts to writing: the role of the participatory, critical subject ("(s)he among the speakers") requires deciphering. This deciphering interlocutor is tantamount to a decoding chatterer. The switching mechanism of the spoken shifts grindingly to the switching mechanism of the written. Benjamin: "In the baroque the tension between the spoken and the written word is immeasurable." The writing of the baroque *Trauerspiel* "does not achieve transcendence by being voiced; rather does the world of written language remain self-sufficient and intent on the display of its own substance. Written language and sound confront each other in tense polarity." The philosophical basis of the allegorical lies in "those comprehensive relationships between the spoken language and script" (*Origin*, 201, 215).

In Benjaminian allegory, writing is a Derridean *supplément*—a substitute for and in excess of spoken language. It is the excessive act that points to a lack in that for which it stands. Writing is other. It is the glyphing of writing—the black marks on the page, the script—in which otherness may reside. Sounded only, writing pretends to be the transparent medium that the rational order requires it to be. Marked, inscribed, encrypted, it becomes something other; there is something hidden and secret beneath its maquillage and manners. "There is nothing subordinate about written script; it is not cast away in reading, like dross. It is absorbed along with what is read, as its 'pattern.' The printers, and indeed the writers of the baroque, paid the closest possible attention to the pattern of the words on the page" (*Origin*, 215). In allegory, words are tattoos: ornamental patterns on the body, ink in [CRYPT]s.

Allegory is the nightmare of Adolf Loos. It is primitive, barbaric; the urge to tattoo is in all of us, he warns, but "we must overcome the Indian in us" (*Spoken into the Void*, 40). Gazing upon the pristine boxes of Loos, we might succumb to a sense of match between his spoken (into the void) and his written (onto the landscape). Until we venture over the threshold. "Every bit as characteristic of [the verse of the baroque Trauerspiel] is the contrast between the logical—if one will, the classicistic—structure of the façade, and the phonetic violence within" (Benjamin, *Origin*, 206). The white box of Loos is a geode: inside there is unbounded sensuality, its "primitivism" shaded by the most transparent of Ruskinian veils. Loos's box and the allegorical box are relatives of Pandora's box, which was not a box at all, but a jug. A sin-build. According to Benjamin keeping the lid on the box brings allegorical language into being. The church's authoritative repression of the pagan (the barbaric), its "banish[ment of] the gods from the memory of the faithful" first gave rise to the allegorical impulse (223). Allegory offers the possibility of a return of the repressed, a writing of what has been imprisoned, in the dark, in the hollow [VESSEL], the void, the jug.

The third, and most intense, intersection lies between Nature and History: "Nature, by now not a reflection of the divine Idea but a structure shared by man, can merge with the history of the entire human species" (Tafuri, *Theories and History,* 82). At this point, we will return to Benjamin's discussion of allegory and symbol. Benjamin turns to Friedrich Creuzer's 1819 work on symbol and myth, *Symbolik und Mythologie der alten Volker, besonders der Griechen,* for insight into the allegorical. And here the concept of time enters the picture. Because of the brevity, or momentariness, of the symbol, it cannot embrace myth as does allegory, which involves progression and series. Benjamin then quotes Görres:

> "We can be perfectly satisfied with the explanation that takes the one [the symbol] as a sign for ideas, which is self-contained, concentrated, and which steadfastly remains itself, while recognizing the other [allegory] as a successively progressing, dramatically mobile, dynamic representation of ideas which has acquired the very fluidity of time. They stand in relation to each other as does the silent, great and mighty natural world of mountains and plants to the living progression of human history." (*Origin,* 165)

"Man's" subjection to nature and the tangential and "enigmatic" questions of the nature of existence and the individual being's biographical historicity coincide here. Death—the ultimate subjection to nature—inscribes the boundary between nature (which is always subject to death and always allegorical) and signifying. Allegory in the baroque Trauerspiel represents a history of signifying nature, analogous to myth in the epic poem of classicism. So, baroque allegory represents a shift of perspective upon signifying nature, that is, a shift from myth to history.

But at this point Benjamin confronts us with a challenge to negotiate the clashing rocks of history and nature: "It is by virtue of a strange combination of nature and history that the allegorical mode of expression is born" (*Origins,* 167). And we track this treacherous itinerary aboard the [HIEROGLYPH]. For in Benjamin the hieroglyph itself marks the emblem of his allegorical journey through knowledge.

It will be important to recall at this point that the maps of Giambattista Piranesi—the drawings of *Il Campo Marzio*—are represented as pictures carved into ancient broken tablets of stone and are thus coded as hieroglyphic maps. Hieroglyphs, those "images of desire that are the non-stuff of which dreams are made" (Taylor, *Altarity*, 240), are ubiquitous in Piranesi's *Vedute di Roma* as well, appearing properly—tattooed—on the shafts of obelisks.

In *Finnegans Wake* there are two proper rebuses, or hieroglyphs, both of which appear in the margins at the close of section II.2 (two point two, which opens with a tattoo: "As we are there are where are we are we there from tomtittot to teetootomtotalitarian. Tea tea too oo" (260.1–3). And in the margin here: "Menly about peebles," the people who are pebbles—the progeny of Deucalion and Pyrrha, the victims of Medusa, caryatids and atlantids, orders, the dead, the petrified [STONE]. This is, after all, the section in which the calculus goes skimming; and an impotent Nietzsche—gotten up in the main text as Giambattista Vico (via the recurring Wagnerian leitmotif of Edgar Quinet, Vico's French propagandist)—Nietzsche, the proponent of eternal returns and breaking up stony words, is invoked in another margin: "Also Spuke Zerothruster" (281.M3). The two rebuses are:

and each is located adjacent to a footnote, augmenting the main text above, which is an allegorical countdown to the close of the section. The final words of II.2 constitute a cryptic [LETTER], a "cryptogam" (words on which we might stumble and break a leg, una gamba, a gam). The letter is called NIGHTLETTER and is from children to parents. It extends "youlldied greedings" and is thus readable as both a Christmas card and an (Oedipal) death wish.

Let us examine the bottom picture. It accompanies the footnote that is marked at the word *geg* in the text. *Geg* appears in the following series: "Aun Do Tri Car Cush Shay Shockt Ockt Ni Geg. Their feed begins," which precedes the NIGHTLETTER. *Geg* represents both "gag" and the number ten in the reverse countdown of this frozen projectile, this zero-thruster, these "autocratic writings of paraboles of famellicurbs" (303.19) that prefigure the landscape of Thomas Pynchon's [ROCKET]ty heterotopia, *Gravity's Rainbow.*[8]

The rebus forms the Roman numeral "X," or ten, a chiasmus, a crossing, a place where something happens. It is the letter "X" of crossing out, of authoritative censorship, and of crossing (transgression), of darkness. It is the night letter. X is the Greek letter *chi,* which stands in for Christ, as in "Xmas." This invokes Joyce's "crossmess parzle," which is *Finnegans Wake* itself: both Christmas parcel and crossword puzzle, it is the near relative of Tafuri's (borrowed) jigsaw puzzle (*gioco di pazienza*) of historical research. X maps an intersection, as in the (rotated) intersection of the *cardo* and *decumanus* or the intersection of the two lives of Oedipus, the point where he took Jocasta's stickpin of glittering stones and jabbed out his eyes. X is an Oedipus map; it is Thomas Pynchon's Oedipa Maas. X marks the (blind) spots of history. X is four V's, or is it two, converging; a T prior to decapitation. X is the mark of Cain, the wanderer, the outcast with blood on his hands. It is the illogical incision made on the bite of the serpent. X is the letter of the repressed, "rated X." X is the monogram of Xanthippe, who poured a pot of piss on the head of her husband, Socrates.

The footnote that accompanies this picture says "And gags for skool and crossbuns and whopes he'll enjoyimsolff over our drawings on the line!" (308.F2). The rebus depicts spanking instruments forming the symbol of poison, the skull and crossbones (with the death's head in absentia). Thus, it is the X of the [PHARMAKON], both poison and cure. Derrida:

> If the pharmakon is "ambivalent," it is because it constitutes the
> medium in which opposites are opposed, the movement and the
> play that links them among themselves, reverses them or makes
> one side cross over into the other (soul/body, good/evil, inside/
> outside, memory/forgetfulness, speech/writing, etc.). . . . We will

watch it infinitely promise itself and endlessly vanish through concealed doorways that shine like mirrors and open onto a labyrinth. It is also this store of deep background that we are calling the pharmacy. (*Dissemination*, 127–128)

This is the promise of Benjaminian allegory and is as well the promise of *Finnegans Wake*. This pharmakon is what the image from which Joyce's rebus is appropriated represents: the alchemical symbol of the hermaphrodite, the crossing of female and male, of the feminine and masculine, of the excremental (the dirty, the bloody) and the precious (the divine), the Philosopher's Stone. The point of X change.

But this rebus is more than a purloined [LETTER]. It is as well *une lettre volée*: please note, it bears vestigial wing tips opposite its club feet.[9] These winglets fly with difficulty, like a [ROCKET] with no thrust, or like Icarus or Lucifer. They bear a remarkable resemblance to the pathetic five-feathered wings of Paul Klee's *Angelus Novus*, a watercolor owned by Walter Benjamin and of which he wrote:

> His face is turned toward the past. Where we perceive a chain of events, he sees one single catastrophe which keeps piling wreckage upon wreckage and hurls it in front of his feet. The angel would like to stay, awaken the dead, and make whole what has been smashed. But a storm is blowing from Paradise; it has got caught in his wings with such violence that the angel can no longer close them. This storm irresistibly propels him into the future to which his back is turned, while the pile of debris before him grows skyward. This storm is what we call progress. (*Illuminations*, 257–258)

The pile of debris, the ruin upon ruin, is what the melancholic Benjamin called history, and here history and the petrified landscape of allegory intersect. This intersection or point of exchange between nature and history encoded in the hieroglyph is articulated a decade after the *Origin of German Tragic Drama* by Benjamin's prodigal son, Theodor W. Adorno. For Adorno, Benjamin's "strange combination of history and nature," entities traditionally held in opposition to each other, is an intersection in which opposition is "transcended." Richard Wolin writes: "According to Adorno, this act of transcendence can be accomplished, given the present constellation of socio-historic forces, *only if each side of the antithesis can be perceived*

as passing over into its opposite" (*Walter Benjamin,* 166; emphasis mine).
So the relation between history and nature must work across a chiasmus,
where "'historical being, in its most extreme historical determinacy, where it
is most historical, is grasped as a natural being' and 'nature, where it apparently hardens itself most thoroughly into nature, is grasped as an historical
being'" (Adorno, quoted in *Walter Benjamin,* 167).

> The Trauerspiel itself figures this chiasmus in Benjamin's text:
> The writer must not conceal the fact that his activity is one of
> arranging, since it was not so much the mere whole as its obvi-
> ously constructed quality that was the principal impression which
> was aimed at. Hence, the display of the craftsmanship . . . shows
> through like the masonry in a building whose rendering has bro-
> ken away. [Here Benjamin marks the intersection of allegory and
> section, the conceptual apparatus of the generative work, with
> its embedded map, a "concept" that also embraces achronologi-
> cal structure: space.] Thus, one might say, nature remained the
> great teacher for the writers of this period. However, nature was
> not seen by them in bud and bloom, but in the over-ripeness and
> decay of her creations. In nature they saw eternal transience, and
> here alone did the saturnine vision of this generation recognize
> history. . . . In the process of decay, and in it alone, the events
> of history shrivel up and become absorbed in the setting. (*Ori-
> gin,* 179)

History meets nature on its backside, the side not that of "an eternal life so much as that of irresistible decay" (*Origin,* 178). This nature,
nature as a stony setting, meets history coming around and collides in the
emblem: "For where nature bears the imprint of history, that is to say where
it is a setting, does it not have a numismatic quality?" (173). This coinlike
quality of having been engraved (of space having been inserted, or thrown
in) distinguishes the emblem, the [HIEROGLYPH], and the ruin. Nature as
setting (nature approaching history) and history as decay (history approaching nature, itself a kind of setting or stage prop against which human nature
plays) coincide in the ruin. It will be important to bear in mind that the ruin
represents a construction in which temporality is a sluggish or slothful opera-
tor, becoming, anachronized, petrified, and thereby legible as spatiality. In
the ruin, the dialectical movements of the Great Dichotomy of space and

time are frozen. The ruin calls the Great Dichotomy into question. (I will pick up this thread again but for the moment leave it dangling.)

In the ruin—the catacombs, the [CRYPT]s—those things that we are desirous of preserving or keeping secret may be buried, or encrypted. Benjamin, quoting Karl Borinski's *Die Antike,* notes: "The enigmatically mysterious character of the effect of the grotesque seems to have been associated with its subterraneanly mysterious origin in buried ruins and catacombs. The word is not derived from *grotta* in the literal sense, but from the 'burial'—in the sense of concealment—which the cave or grotto expresses" (*Origin,* 171).

Here Benjamin is doubling: the quotation refers to the concept of the grotesque in antiquity, the "secret storehouse of invention" (171) of baroque allegory. So the grotesque is the burial place of secret things that drive allegory, and in this way it relates to hieroglyphic script, which performs similarly. At this point, script and crypt enjoy a confluence, which will be called *scrypt,* a signifier for this hole, this writing of something that is empty space, where something secret or sacred—something unspeakable or unrepresentable—is kept, a holey space.[10]

The intersection of allegory and the grotesque in Benjamin marks the beginning of a significant itinerary. Writing out of and upon the grotesque body of Georges Bataille, in particular Bataille's "tube with two orifices, which bears ramificatory complications that call interiority-exteriority distinctions into question, Mark Taylor indicates that

> this chiasmic body cannot be articulated in terms of the binary
> opposites that structure thought and language. Never "proper,
> clean, neat, or tidy," the body is inescapably transgressive. . . . In
> examining [sperm, menstrual blood, urine, fecal matter, vomit,
> tears, sobs, screams, cries and laughter], Bataille develops a sca-
> tology through which he attempts to subvert the eschatology of
> speculative philosophy and traditional theology. [Here Taylor in-
> serts a note, reminding us of "the use of the word 'altar' to refer
> to a toilet."] While Hegel is preoccupied with securing the Sys-
> tem "proper" by wiping or flushing away *Kote* [THE PROPER],
> Bataille struggles to expose the gap through which the repressed
> eternally returns. (*Altarity,* 126)

The grotesque body is the body of crypts, invaginations and folds—of secret voids, burial chambers where secrets and sacreds may be preserved. In this body, nature, history, theology, and psychoanalysis slide around and in and out of each other in utter indistinguishability.

The chiasmic body is a [HIEROGLYPH]ic text. It represents the unrepresentable (the unspeakable): the hissing holes "through which the repressed eternally returns." An illegible text. Benjamin likens baroque allegory to texts written in intertwined Egyptian, Greek, and Christian pictorial languages; it offered a place where theology could preserve the power of sacred things (by embedding them in the profane). This kind of writing was also capable of providing "a refuge for many ideas which people were reluctant to voice openly before princes" (*Origin,* 172).

Fredric Jameson has noted this capability of allegory in the literature of what he generalizes as "the third world": "All third-world texts are necessarily, I want to argue, allegorical, and in a very specific way: they are to be read as what I will call *national allegories*" ("Third-World Literature," 69).[11] Jameson suggests that in these allegorical texts the gap between the libidinal (personal, private, unconscious) and the political (collective, world of classes), a major determining characteristic of capitalist culture, is erased; he emphasizes that in "third-world" texts (his examples are primarily African and Chinese), *"the story of the private individual destiny is always an allegory of the embattled situation of the public third-world culture and society"* (69). Jameson here locates allegory as the place where ideas repressed by the dominant might be hidden, as well as the place where the personal and political may coincide. Reading such allegories requires a "new [MAPPING] process" in which "we must rethink our conventional conception of the symbolic levels of narrative (where sexuality and politics might be in homology to each other, for instance) as a set of loops or circuits which intersect and overdetermine each other" (73). These allegories, in distinction to what Jameson labels "the unconscious allegories of our own ["first-world"] cultural texts," are "conscious and overt" (79–80). What Jameson's text suggests (albeit obliquely) for present purposes is the potential of allegory as a vehicle for the return of any repressed. Jameson's concept of "mapping," of which "national allegory" is a form, is "structurally available to the dominated rather than the dominating classes" (88*n*26).

[MAPPING]

The midden heap—the emblematic dumping ground in *Finnegans Wake*—is a mapping of the [HEN]'s [LETTER]: *une lettre volée,* both obvious and hidden, and not legible to all in the same way. The little biddies can scratch up the most wee ("tea tea too oo") bits.[12]

Benjamin quotes Martin Opitz: "Because the earliest rude world was too crude and uncivilised and people could not therefore correctly grasp and understand the teachings of wisdom and heavenly things, wise men had to conceal and bury what they had discovered for the cultivation of the fear of God, morality, and good conduct, in rhymes and fables, to which the common people are disposed to listen" (*Origin,* 172). That which is hidden in the allegorical is theological, the sacred buried in the profane. This is what is hidden in the Trauerspiel, suggests Bataille: "TRAGEDY, like a festival given in honor of horror-spreading TIME, depicted for gathered men the signs of delirium and death whereby they might recognize their true nature" (*Visions of Excess,* 218). But this aspect has been carved away—properly—from religion, now a cagey structure of domination. Taylor:

> Bataille maintains that art now provides a more effective access to the uncanny time-space of the sacred. . . . In *Lascaux, or the Birth of Art,* he argues that art "begins" in the bowels of mother earth. . . . From the beginning (if indeed there is a beginning), there is something *grotto-esque* and *dirty* about art. Bataille is convinced that the dirt of art's grotesque, subterranean "origin" can never be wiped away. Art, like religion, emerges from the filth of the sacred. (*Altarity,* 141–142)

We might add architecture, "the mother of the arts," with its origins as alternative to the cave. And if we choose to give credence to George Hersey's thesis that the ornamentation of classical temples was a miming of the accoutrements and residue of ritual sacrifice (as the gory things were hung within the sacrificial grove), architecture actually *represents* the "filth of the sacred" (see Hersey, *Lost Meaning*).

Art's (and architecture's) emergence [MIRROR]s the merging (albeit a collisive one) in the Trauerspiel, as Bataille's effective erasure of the dialectic mirrors Benjamin's invocation of it. (The dialectic prepares the way for its own dissolution, after all. The introduction of mediation makes it possible to throw the whole business into question.) Allegory in Benjamin, like the Dionysian orgy in Bataille, is a "harsh disturbance of the peace and a disruption of law and order" (*Origin*, 177), which occurs at the place where the sacred and the profane are indistinguishable. And this place is allegorizable (or emblematizable) by allegory itself. Because in allegory "any person, any object, any relationship can mean absolutely anything else"; the profane (material) world becomes a place in which each person, object, or relationship is of no particular significance. At the same time, these things that are used to signify acquire a power that makes them then different, locates them on a higher plane, that is, renders them sacred. "Considered in allegorical terms, the profane world is both elevated and devalued." Benjamin's dialectic is echoed in the dialectic of convention and expression. Allegory is, again, both. "Here too the solution is a dialectical one. It lies in the essence of writing itself" (175). Allegory thus connects to criticism, both convention of expression ("like every kind of writing") and expression of convention. "The strategy of criticism is located in the object of criticism" as "the allegorical work tends to prescribe the direction of its own commentary" (Serres, *Hermes*, 38; Owens, "Allegorical Impulse," 69). The Trauerspiel is an object with no outer form: "Its outer form has died away" (*Origin*, 182). An intricately constructed ruin of "extraordinary detail," petrified, mortified. "Criticism means the mortification of works" (182). This returns allegory (complex, timeless, hieroglyph script) to its position of opposition to the symbol (simple, fleeting, transparent image), where "in it the baroque reveals itself to be the sovereign opposite of classicism." Allegory, which "at one stroke . . . transforms things and works into stirring writing" (176), thereby resting on an unstable ground "between sacred standing and profane comprehensibility" (175), is a stormy "synthesis" reached "as a result of the conflict between theological and artistic intentions, a synthesis not so much in the sense of a peace as a *treuga dei* between the conflicting opinions" (177).

Allegory is associated with the melancholic. "For the only pleasure the melancholic permits himself, and it is a powerful one, is allegory" (*Origin*, 185). The gaze of melancholy causes life (time) to flow out of objects— petrifies them—so that they remain, dead but preserved. Melancholy is the attribute of Saturn, or Cronos (who castrated his father and brother, Uranus, birthing Aphrodite from the blood [PHARMAKON]), the dualistic god of extremes. One of the forgotten symbols of melancholy, Benjamin points out, is the [STONE], which is also (for reasons we have seen) an allegorical emblem par excellence. "He was by nature pensive and of a melancholy complexion, which dispositions ponder a matter more constantly and proceed more cautiously in all their actions. Neither the serpent-headed Medusa, nor the African monster, nor the weeping crocodile of this world could mislead his gaze, still less transform his limbs into an unfeeling stone" (154).

[MAPPING]

When Giambattista Vico was a tiny child, he fell off a ladder head first, incurring near-fatal injury. According to Vico, it was this fall that set his own *natura malinconica,* the philosopher's temperament (*Autobiography,* 111).

"Melancholy betrays the world for the sake of knowledge," claims Vico (*Autobiography,* 157). The melancholic, the allegorist, gazes into a "bottomless pit of contemplation" (231). Let me appropriate Owens' citation of the artist Robert Smithson here:

> The names of minerals and the minerals themselves do not differ from each other, because at the bottom of both the material and the print is the beginning of an abysmal number of fissures. Words and rocks contain a language that follows a syntax of splits and ruptures. Look at any word long enough and you will see it open up into a series of faults, into a terrain of particles each containing its own void. ("Allegorical Impulse," 85)

Near the end of his text, Benjamin leaves us with a final dialectic of allegory, so that it does not,

> as those who lose their footing through somersaults in their fall, . . . fall from emblem to emblem down into the dizziness of its bottomless depths. . . . Ultimately in the death-signs of the baroque the direction of allegorical reflection is reversed; on the second part of its wide arc it returns, to redeem. . . . These allegories fill out and deny the void in which they are represented, just as, ultimately, the intention does not faithfully rest in the contemplation of bones, but faithlessly leaps forward to the idea of resurrection. (*Origin,* 232–233)

Six Potato

The geography of *Finnegans Wake* is a petrified corpse, the body of the Dead Father. James Joyce's friend and publisher Sylvia Beach affectionately called him "Melancholy Jesus," and his wife, Nora Barnacle, called him "good-for-nothing" (sloth and dullness are characteristics of the melancholic). The melancholic's passion is knowledge, which Benjamin associates with evil. ("One demon knows more than you.") Recall that knowledge is associated with evil in the Bible. Benjamin notes that the attribute of Adam is melancholy and the attribute of Eve is joyfulness. He also points out the problem with this duality: madness is associated with melancholy, but Eve instigates the Fall (*Origin,* 147). The only way out of this conundrum is to call Benjamin's division into question. Eve, after all, first consumed the evil knowledge, the secret knowledge of the sacred and profane. Eve, born of Medusa, with her melancholic's stony gaze and her intimacy with serpents. Eve, who bore two sons, Cain and Abel, the passionate, murderous wanderer (Cain was his mother's son) and the gentle, obedient favorite of God. Cain and Abel, who in *Finnegans Wake* appear as Shem and Shaun, the sons of the petrified landscape, Humphrey Chimpden Earwicker, and the flowing, disseminative river, Anna Livia Plurabelle. Shem, the Penman, is his mother's son: a sinister writer, he is always blaspheming, with "an artificial tongue with a natural curl" (169.15–16). Shem lives in the House O'Shame (the "Haunted Inkbottle") where he is "an ineleuctable phantom . . . writing the mystery of himself in furniture" (184.8–10). Shaun, the Postman, is a man's man: rational, right, orderly, "dogmestic," "decent," "gracious," and, notably, "able."

Shem is perhaps nowhere more present than in the fifteen-hundred-word sentence occupying pages 119 to 123 that confuses the act of writing and the "vaulting feminine libido," which is, in the end, "sternly controlled and easily repersuaded by the uniform matteroffactness of a meandering male fist" (123.8–10).

[MAPPING]

When we are geographically distant, my lover constructs my body with imagery, aestheticizes—lips, breasts, eyes, curves, colors. Medusa is a masculine projection. The voyeur petrifies the body. (What does it look like?) I, eyeless and with no aegis, map the deep surfaces of his body with the memory of the tongue, or of the skin. I write his body with dark, olfactory ink, from scalp to armpit to groin to behind the knee to between the toes. I trace the complex of nuances among these points of intensity. I write the feminine.[13] An un-visible tattoo. When it (*jouissance*) comes to (bleeds into) architecture, what it looks like hardly matters. The distant pleasures of the voyeur are pale as ice in the presence of the *scrypteuse*. The *ombre elle*.

Question: What has eyes but cannot see?

The Penman is a chatterer. (Remove the "ise" from P. Eisenman and see what you get.)[14] Also the possessor of peculiar tattoos: "the first till last alshemist wrote over every square inch of the only foolscap available, his own body, till by its corrosive sublimation one continuous present tense integument slowly unfolded all marryvoising moodmoulded cyclewheeling history" (185.34–186.2).

Shem is "middayevil." Benjamin: "In their supreme, western, form the mosaic and the treatise are products of the Middle Ages; it is their very real affinity which makes comparison possible" (*Origin*, 29).

Shem writes, Shaun delivers. Shaun and Shem appear in the *Wake* as Same and Th'other: both the twins of Plato and Thamous, regal representative of Amon Ra, the sun god who creates by speaking, and Thoth, the inventor of writing, a "cure" for memory loss, which is rejected (as a poison) by Thamous [HEN, PHARMAKON].[15] Hélène Cixous: "Shaun boasts of being the possessor of all words as he is the master of all men, and thus establishes his allegiance to capitalism and patriarchy" (*Exile of Joyce*, 743). Fredric Jameson's happy typo in "Postmodernism, or the Cultural Logic of Late Capitalism," is telling here. ("Who has known how to metamorphose a 'typo' proper to protect the one with a slip into which the other can fall?"; Derrida, *Post Card*, 515) After noting the commercial failure that is due to the inability of shoppers to find the boutiques in John Portman's Westin Bonaventure Hotel in Los Angeles, Jameson writes: "When you recall that *Postman* is a businessman as well as an architect, and a millionaire developer, an artist who is at one and the same time a capitalist in his own right, one cannot but feel that here too something of a 'return of the repressed' is involved" (83; emphasis mine).[16]

The Postman gazes into the depths of a glassy surface and sees his reflection [MIRROR], just as did Narcissus, who spurned Echo, the ceaseless chatterer. The Penman sees into the abysmal liquid, the void, the Pandora's jug [VESSEL]. Th'other speaks with stylish instrument.

In *Finnegans Wake,* Shem and Shaun are unstable as individuals. They flow in and out of each other; they are always becoming. There is always difference, but it will not hold still. It is mercurial. "The [PHAR-MAKON] always penetrates like a liquid; it is absorbed, drunk, introduced into the inside, which it first marks with the hardness of the type, soon to invade it and inundate it with its medicine, its brew, its drink, its potion, its poison. In liquid, opposites are more easily mixed. Liquid is the element of the pharmakon" (Derrida, "Plato's Pharmacy," *Dissemination,* 152). Liquid is the matrix of the mosaic: it bleeds among the [STONE]s; it separates them and holds them together.

> Just as mosaics preserve their majesty despite their fragmentation into capricious particles, so philosophical contemplation is not lacking in momentum. Both are made up of the distinct and the disparate; and nothing could bear more powerful testimony to the transcendent force of the sacred image and the truth itself. The value of fragments of thought is all the greater the less direct their relationship to the underlying idea, and the brilliance of the representation depends as much on this value as the brilliance of the mosaic does on the quality of the glass paste. (Benjamin, *Origin,* 28–29)

Seven Potato

My daughter Sarah, who is eight[17] and wants to be a writer when she grows up, has brought me her latest production, a "book for little kids" called *The Pattern Book and Other.* This book contains information that Sarah, the Diderot of the third grade, deems it necessary for little kids like her four-year-old cousin Kate to know. The book consists of four chapters:

> Chapter I: "Patterns." A mosaic (with obscene glue globs display-ing themselves shamelessly) of colored paper patterns in circles, squares, triangles, and ellipses.
> Chapter II: "Math." An illustrated $2 + 2 = 4$, $4 + 4 = 8$.

Chapter III: "Knock-Knock Jokes." ("Knock Knock." "Who's there?" "Banana," and so on.)

Chapter IV: "Meshering." (Includes the fact that there are "four quarks in a galleon.")

It astounds me that that which I labor so hard to understand is mere, and pure, child's play. Children perhaps know the untruth of the mantra that we teach them. Children (those little nomadic androgynes that we carve away at from the moment they come into the world) know, as Nietzsche knew, that words, the wall material of the symbolic order, are as likely to break our bones (our matrix) [18] as are sticks and stones. And the constructions (historical, philosophical) they embody are as present, as familiar, as beloved, as oppressive, and as cold and pale as the architectural constructions which stand for them.

In Wim Wenders' film *Wings of Desire,* only Peter Falk, playing a simulacrum of himself—an actor known for playing a bumbling, babbling, one-eyed detective who occupies his spare time making drawings—but also playing the ghost of what the protagonist-angel is to become (an *Angelus Novus*), and the children, the little chattering magpies, understand such constructions. The chiasmus of the film, the place where the angel's blood flows red (where the image shifts from black and white to Technicolor), occurs at the Berlin wall, a wall made of pure—or is it mere—ideology.[19]

More

In writing of collage and allegory, the realm of both Walter Benjamin and Jacques Derrida, Gregory Ulmer cites Derrida on the resulting undecidability of reading the assembly that is a collage. Each heterogeneous element, or detail, of the collage, because of its position both as a fragment that can be connected to its original context and as a part of a new whole, shuttles between "presence and absence," and thus disallows a linear or univocal reading of the whole ("Object of Post-Criticism," 88).

Naomi Schor addresses the undecidability engendered by allegorical detail:

> The detail with an allegorical vocation is distinguished by its "oversignification" (Baudrillard); this is not a matter of realism, but of surrealism, if not hyperrealism. Finally, the allegorical de-

tail is a disproportionately enlarged ornamental detail; bearing the seal of transcendence, it testifies to the loss of all transcendental signifieds in the modern period. In short, the modern allegorical detail is a parody of the traditional theological detail. It is the detail deserted by God. . . . The allegorical detail is a disembodied and destabilized detail. (*Reading in Detail,* 61)

The phenomenon cited by Schor and labeled oversignification by Baudrillard is one of the mechanisms of Derrida's *gram,* which is to grammatology what the sign is to semiology. One of the corollaries of the gram as Derrida approaches it is the notion of the *supplément:* an entity added to another entity that is both in excess of that to which it is added—is excessive—and that, by nature of being added, points to, by supplying, a lack in the original entity. Ulmer notes that Craig Owens identified allegory with the supplément, and thus with writing, in its supplementarity to speech. Walter Benjamin made this identification long before, when he connected baroque allegory with hieroglyphs and other forms of script.

In addressing objections to the possibility of sustaining the distinction that Owens made, and that Derrida's projects suggest, between the self-referential (through metaphor) image of modernism and the problematized reference of postmodernism, Ulmer rescues from the realm of formalism grammatology and, more significant here, the notion of allegory articulated and used by Benjamin and Derrida:

Grammatology has emerged on the far side of the formalist crisis and developed a discourse which is fully referential, but referential in the manner of "narrative allegory" rather than of "allegoresis." "Allegoresis," the mode of commentary long practiced by traditional critics, "suspends" the surface of the text, applying a terminology of "verticalness, levels, hidden meaning, the hieratic difficulty of interpretation," whereas "narrative allegory" (practiced by post-critics) explores the literal—[LETTER]al—level of the language itself, in a horizontal investigation of the polysemous meanings simultaneously available in the words themselves—in etymologies and puns—and in the things the words name. . . . In short, narrative allegory *favors the material of the signifier over the meanings of the signifieds.* ("Object of Post-Criticism," 95; emphasis mine)

With this distinction between conventional allegory and the allegory of Joyce, Benjamin, Derrida, and Piranesi, Ulmer also opens a door to architecture. As we explore these possibilities in architecture, with its grand and enduring, however limited, canon of symbolic materiality, we are once again *shuttling:* maintaining the veiled or layered possibilities of allegoresis while playing over them at the level of detail with the tools of narrative allegory (a dissemination upon an emplotment). The construction of such an architecture mirrors the constructions of Joyce and Piranesi.

Chapter 2

Three

Constructions

Construction One: *Il Campo Marzio:*
"La région où s'érige le désir sans contrainte"

The great difficulties in understanding the language . . . not . . .
from an inability to read the script, every letter of which is now
clearly understood. It is as if books were discovered, printed in
our own Roman letters, so that one could articulate the words
without trouble, but written in an unknown language with no
known parallels.

Ellen Macnamara, *Everyday Life of the Etruscans,*
cited by Rachel DuPlessis in *The Pink Guitar* (ellipses in original)

Order is, at one and the same time, that which is given in all
things as their inner law, the hidden network that determines the
way they confront one another, and also that which has no existence except in the grid created by a glance, an examination, a
language; and it is only in the blank spaces of this grid that order
manifests itself in depth as though already there, waiting in silence
for the moment of its expression.

Michel Foucault, *The Order of Things*

In the autumn of 1757, Giovanni Battista Piranesi completed a
postscript to his previously published *Antichità Romane.* The six contiguous
plates depict an arrangement of stone fragments on which are incised a master plan of the *Campo Marzio.* The fragments appear to be the remains of a

plan of ancient Rome, the footprints of layer upon layer of antique Roman buildings. A few diagrams leap out in familiarity: here the Pantheon, there the Theater of Marcellus, and the Piazza Navona; the Mausoleum of Hadrian (the Castello Sant'Angelo) sits in its proper place beside the Tiber, which snakes through the drawing in its "tibertine" way. Upon closer inspection, however, the reader of the drawing will find that it bears little resemblance to any factually recorded reality, either of ancient Rome or of eighteenth-century Rome, although it continues to look distinctly Roman and certainly ancient.

Or does it?

[MAPPING]
The Warp, The Walls:
Fragment
The City
The Wall
The River
The Gate to the Underworld
The Seasonal Clock
Collision

Fragment
The idea of fragment is not an idea of origin. Fragment demands a preceding action. The act is collision; the object is fragment. The cause is collision; the effect is fragment. Implied is the shattering of a whole. The shattered whole is a synthetic whole (although it may appear to be an analytic whole of additive parts), in which the shattering is the mechanism of the syntax.

> Whether in the order of spoken or written discourse, no element can function as a sign without referring to another element which itself is not simply present. This inter[WEAVING] results in each "element"—phoneme or grapheme—being constituted on the basis of the trace within it of the other elements of the chain or system. This interweaving, this textile, is the text produced only in the transformation of another text. Nothing, neither among the

Detail from Giovanni Battista Piranesi, *Il Campo Marzio dell'Antica Roma: Ichnographia* (1762)

elements nor within the system, is anywhere ever simply present or absent. There are only, everywhere, differences and traces of traces. (Jacques Derrida, *Positions*)[1]

The classically disposed spirits no less than those romantically inclined—as these two species always exist—carry a vision of the future: but the former out of a strength of their time; the latter, out of its weakness. (Friedrich Nietzsche, "The Wanderer and His Shadow")

Piranesi looked about and found, to his horror, the impassive cage of the Cartesian-Newtonian universe descending onto his world. The *Campo Marzio Ichnographia* is a product of his reaction. The drawing represents the real and the unreal, the past and the future, a place and no place. With it, Piranesi shatters history and geography, time and space. The device is critical. It is allegorical. Piranesi's construction of architectural bits, the sediment of history, corresponds to the fractured narrative of James Joyce's *Ulysses*.

[MAPPING]

1762 Publication of *Il Campo Marzio del'Antica Roma*.

1756 Publication of *Antichità Romane*, lauding Roman genius for construction, opposing Winckelmann.

1755 Publication of Johann Joachim Winckelmann's influential essay extolling the virtues of Greek art and advocating its use as a spring-board for contemporary art.

1753 James Stuart and Nicholas Revett propose an expedition to the Aegean to find the "source" (Greek) of art.

1753 Paris publication of the Abbaye Laugier's *Essai sur l'architecture,* defending Greek architecture as the source of indisputable, rational (Newtonian) principles of architecture [HOUSE, THE PROPER].

Il Campo Marzio del' Antica Roma was a polemical weapon in the eighteenth-century battle over the appropriate origin of good architecture. With the forms it represents, it names Etruria, not Greece, as the source of Roman architecture.

1725 Publication of *La Scienza Nuova,* the major work of Giambattista Vico, a Neapolitan philosopher of history and critic of the Cartesian theory of knowledge.

Resemblances, according to Foucault, require a signature in order to be observable. One signature marking the resemblance of the work of Piranesi, the eighteenth-century architect, to that of Joyce, the twentieth-century writer, belongs to Vico. Vico's disjointed collection of ideas sought to represent the world by a method that looked to myth as explanation and to language as archaeological evidence. Vico concluded that the sources of Roman institutions were Etruscan.

ANTHROPOLOGY 3, HISTORY 0.

Lévi-Strauss has declared that he is not responsible for his books: they get written through him. (Rodney Needham, review of *Le Regard éloigné*)

I shall remain in Borges, not in myself (if it is true that I am someone), but I recognize myself less in his books than in many others or in the laborious strumming of a guitar. Years ago I tried to free myself from him and went from the mythologies of the suburbs to the games with time and infinity, but those games belong to Borges now and I shall have to imagine other things. . . . I do not know which of us has written this page. (Jorge Luis Borges, "Borges and I")

The *Campo Marzio Ichnographia* is, in a sense, surreal. It anticipates the poem-objects of André Breton, which juxtapose real and unreal, remembered known and imagined unknown, in an irritating, provocative manner. Like the surrealist object, it is partial; it is the result of a collision. As in the surrealist object, the collision is born in the brain of the maker, a collision that the reader seeks and makes again; for collisions constitute the language. But, regarded again, both Piranesi and Joyce depart radically from surrealism, and their work represents in fact exactly that from which Breton and his colleagues recoiled. Although much of the communicating mechanism operates from the unconscious (in a kind of reverse automatism), a reading of the texts of Piranesi and Joyce requires associations—switching mechanisms—based upon a knowledge of the conscious, national world of ideas.

There must be in the nature of human institutions a mental language common to all nations which uniformly grasps the substance of things feasible in human social life and expresses it with as many diverse modifications as these same things may have diverse aspects. (Giambattista Vico, *La Scienza Nuova*)

Piranesi's drawing prefigures *Ulysses* and *Finnegans Wake* in its overt display of Vico's influence, through its armature using the city as labyrinth/as marker of something greater/as built and ordered upon collective mythmaking, and, most significant, in its palimpsestic, [PATCHWORK]like form. The city in both Joyce and Piranesi is an intricate network of sites of interpretation.

[MAPPING]

The Weft, The Way: *Shevirath hakelim*, the breaking-apart-of-the-vessels.

The City

Piranesi's drawing maps a city, both a real city (Rome) and a city located in a geography of the imagination,[2] a city that represents something other. Like Freud's use of "The Eternal City" as a metaphor for the human brain, Piranesi's Rome points to the presence of (hidden, secreted, [CRYPT]ic) elements of prehistory—the primitive, the mythical—in the Rome of any moment.

> The city, however, does not tell its past, but contains it like the lines of a hand, written in the corners of the streets, the gratings of the windows, the banisters of the steps, the antennae of the lightning rods, the poles of the flags, every segment marked in turn with scratches, indentations, scrolls. (Italo Calvino, *Invisible Cities*)

But Piranesi's city is not only marked; it is also marker. It marks the labyrinth of the underworld, which is the lowermost layer of its palimpsest, as well as that of the overworld, the universe.

Vico's axiom "The order of ideas follows the order of institutions" (sec. 238), lays the foundation for his idea of poetic wisdom, which in turn supports his poetic geography. Poetic wisdom, the discovery of the unknown through the known (the words of the theological poets), relies on the theory

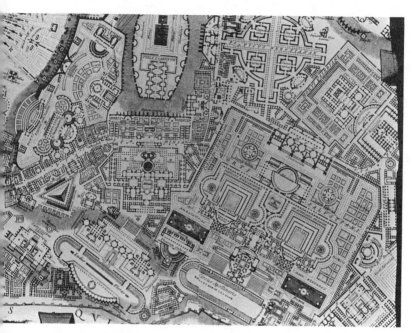

Detail from Giovanni Battista Piranesi, *Il Campo Marzio dell'Antica Roma: Ichnographia* (1762)

that the fabulous must have some basis in fact. Through poetic geography, Vico demonstrated the connection between the legendary city of Troy and the founding of the city of Rome (secs. 770–773).

> Dardans with applause
> Now greeted the shy boys and loved their show,
> Marking in each the features of his forebears.
> After the troop had circled his assembly
> Before their families' eyes, Epytides
> From the wings shouted an order prearranged
> And cracked his whip. The column split apart
> As files in the three squadrons all in line
> Turned away, cantering left and right; recalled,
> They wheeled and dipped their lances for a charge.
> They entered then on parades and counter-parades,
> The two detachments, matched in the arena,
> Winding in and out of one another,
> And whipped into sham cavalry skirmishes
> By basing backs in flight, then whirling round
> With leveled points, then patching up a truce
> And riding side by side. So intricate
> In ancient times on mountainous Crete they say
> The Labyrinth, between walls in the dark,
> Ran criss-cross a bewildering thousand ways
> Devised by guile, a maze insoluble,
> Breaking down every clue to the way out [GAME].
> So intricate the drill of Trojan boys
> Who wove the patterns of their pacing horses
> Figured, in sport, retreats and skirmishes—
> Like dolphins in the drenching sea, Carpathian
> Or Libyan, that shear through waves in play.
> This mode of drill, this mimicry of war,
> Ascanius brought back in our first years
> When he walled Alba Longa; and he taught
> The ancient Latins to perform the drill
> As he had done with other Trojan boys.
> The Albans taught their children, and in turn

Great Rome took up this glory of the founders.

The boys are called Troy now, the whole troop Trojan.[3]

(Virgil, *Aeneid,* book 5, trans. Robert Fitzgerald)

Vico's poetic geography also suggests that the beginnings of the Cretan labyrinth lie in the configuration of the islands in the Aegean Sea, that is, the real world of the Greeks. Homer's clashing rocks, which shattered passing ships to bits, come from this uncharted, and, therefore, labyrinthine, world.

> Here . . . we see a reason for regarding this episode ["The Wandering Rocks"] as the microcosm of the universe of *Ulysses,* inspired by its creator with the breath of life, yet fashioned by the practised hand of an artificer, maker of labyrinths: a living labyrinth. (Stuart Gilbert, *James Joyce's* Ulysses)

In the geography of the imagination, the world of ideas is a labyrinth in which the imagination is a kind of reverse Ariadne's thread, by which one is led into the labyrinth. The realm of ideas is analogous to what for the ancients was the Aegean Sea and to what for Vico was history: a labyrinth. When that realm has been charted, however, it can no longer be represented by a labyrinth; the labyrinth must slide to another place. Foucault's view of knowledge as a collection of colliding and intersecting grids (clashing grids, wandering grids) offers this kind of place. We can wander here; we often return to familiar points, familiar intersections, which give pleasure. This is the mythical labyrinth, which we enter and from which, we discover, we have no desire to emerge.

> The Library is a sphere whose exact center is any one of its hexagons and whose circumference is inaccessible. (Jorge Luis Borges, "The Library of Babel")

> The Vico Road goes round and round to meet where terms begin. (James Joyce, *Finnegans Wake*)

A "VICOUS CIRCLE": From fragment as telos to the Absolute as telos.

A POSSIBILITY: There is only one idea and the blind poet recorded it.

> Among the Immortals . . . every act (and every thought) is the echo of others that preceded it in the past, with no visible begin-

Illustration of the Trojan Game. Carved drawing on the tragliatella jug.

ning, or the faithful presage of others that in the future will repeat it to a vertiginous degree. There is nothing that is not as if lost in a maze of indefatigable mirrors. Nothing can happen only once, nothing is preciously precarious. The elegiacal, the serious, the ceremonial, do not hold for the Immortals. Homer and I separated at the gates of Tangier. I think we did not even say goodbye. (Jorge Luis Borges, "The Immortal")

The generating structure of the *Campo Marzio, Ulysses,* and *Finnegans Wake* is a labyrinth, and, with its concentric walls, it resembles the concentric spheres of universe, the circles of the lower world, and the mediating microcosm, the city, which in its archetypal form—Troy or Jericho—consists of encircling walls.

Although Piranesi's city-labyrinth is viewed from far above (a god's eye view) and Joyce's modern city-labyrinth is experienced from a man's eye view, each may be characterized by the distancing from its ostensible subject that comes from a stance deep within the mind of its creator. José Ortega y Gasset, in "On the Point of View in the Arts," writes that this "distant vision" (which is in reality more proximate than the "proximate vision" of a Renaissance painting) characterizes modern art (*Dehumanization of Art,* 109–110). Piranesi's distant vision of a Rome that is and is not Rome, of the remembered and the imagined, is peculiarly modern.

Throughout his work Joyce puts Jack at the center of the house he built, Daedalus at the center of the labyrinth, from which the design spirals out or radiates. . . . *Finnegans Wake* is the [HOUSE] that Jack Joyce built. (Guy Davenport, "The House That Jack Built")

This is the Hausman all paven and stoned, that cribbed the Cabin that never was owned that cocked his leg and hennad his Egg [UNDESIRABLE BEASTS]. (James Joyce, *Finnegans Wake*)

The Wall

What we see when we look at the *Campo Marzio Ichnographia* are representations of the vestiges of walls—ancient city walls, walls of buildings, garden walls—the structure of the city. What we see when we look at a labyrinth are its walls. In the labyrinth, the walls are the presence, but the

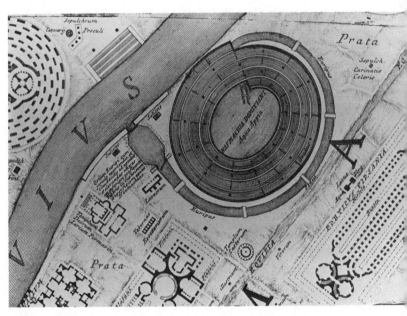

Detail from Giovanni Battista Piranesi, *Il Campo Marzio dell'Antica Roma:
Ichnographia* (1762)

walls are not the substance. Only the space captured by the walls, the way, occupies the wanderer.

Boustrophedon, the "ox turns in plowing," is a formal representation of discourse, writing that runs in two different directions. What is not the form—the turning—may be seen as the spaces between the turnings, or as one great entity surrounding the form. Boustrophedon is a sign of discourse existing in tropological space, in a field of tropes, of turnings. When the boustrophedon is elaborated, is at intervals rotated upon itself, it suggests a labyrinth (compare it to the Trojan [GAME]). It remains a form existing in the field or space, but it captures a part of that field or space in its enfoldments.

The activity of Ulysses is essentially Viconian; that of Penelope tends to the Cartesian. He wanders; she weaves and unravels. His world is a labyrinth; hers is a grid. His, the unknown; hers, the known. For Ulysses, only the way is significant. For Penelope, only the structure of her object is important. It is constructed each time according to the same principles, and dismantled each time according to the same principles. Warp continuous; ninety-degree weft woven in—back and forth, in the form of boustrophedon—and raveled out. The process is modular and repetitive. Sometimes new threads are introduced, but they are treated no differently from the old, used, and reused threads [WEAVING, PATCHWORK]. Penelope renders myth frozen in the name of Euclid, earth measurer. Ulysses, like Piranesi, earth tracer, wanders parts of worlds in which myth is the present condition [MAPPING].

But Penelope is a daughter of Metis.[4] She is an ambiguous source of truth and falsehood. She is not to be categorized nor dismissed so readily. She is the emblem, the eccentric center, the connector. Her act appears "proper" [THE PROPER], but it presents the unspeakable. Her act is a model for that to which this construction aspires.

> A bag of the blues for Funny Fitz; a *Missa pro Messa* for Taff de Taff; Jill, the spoon of a girl, for Jack, the broth of a boy; a Rogerson Crusoe's Friday fast for Caducus Angelus Rubiconstein; three hundred and sixtysix poplin tyne for revery warp in the weaver's woof for Victor Hugonot. (James Joyce, *Finnegans Wake*)

The River

Across the broken slab flows the Tiber, backbone of the city, and backbone of the drawing. It is an element represented and representing, a river and a model of narrative, looping through a fiction of space, its lace apron[5] of tributaries and canals bound into the tapestry of the city.

> In Esmeralda, city of water, a network of canals span and intersect each other. To go from one place to another you have always the choice between land and boat: and since the shortest distance between two points in Esmeralda is not a straight line but a zigzag that ramifies in tortuous optimal routes, the ways that open to each passerby are never two, but many, and they increase further for those who alternate a stretch by boat with one on dry land.
>
> (Italo Calvino, *Invisible Cities*)

The river marks the point of transition from the world to the underworld. It is passage, both in the spatial sense of a medium of passage from one realm to another and in the temporal sense of flow.[6] The river (of time, of history) denotes the boundary between the labyrinth of life and the labyrinth of death.

Invoking the theological poets, Vico acknowledges the river boundary in his "Poetic Cosmography": Diana, the first deity to be associated with the perennial springs (which the poets called Styx) of the lower world, was a tripartite goddess who, in her three forms, bounded and linked the three worlds of the heavens, the earth, and the underworld. As Diana, Cynthia, and Hecate (with over/undertones of Proserpina), the water deity provided a passage among worlds.

> Well, arundgirond in a waveney lyne aringarouma she pattered and swung and sidled, dribbling her boulder through narrowa mosses, the diliskydrear on our drier side and the vilde vetchvine agin us, curara here, careero there, not knowing which medway or weser to strike it, edereider, making chattahoochee all to her ain chichiu, like Santa Claus at the cree of the pale and puny, nistling to hear for their tiny hearties, her arms encircling Isolabella, then running with reconciled Romas and Reims, on like a lech to be off like a dart, then bathing Dirty Hans' spatters with spittle, with a Christmas box apiece for aisch and iveryone of her childer, the

Detail from Giovanni Battista Piranesi, *Il Campo Marzio dell'Antica Roma: Ichnographia* (1762)

birthday gifts they dreamt they gabe her, the spoiled she fleetly laid at our door! . . . for Saara Philpot a jordan vale tearorne; a pretty box of Pettyfib's Powder for Eileen Aruna to whiten her teeth and outflash Helen Arhone; a whippingtop for Eddy Lawless; for Kitty Coleraine of Butterman's Lane a penny wise for her foolish pitcher; a putty shovel for Terry the Puckaun; an apotamus mask for Promoter Dunne; a niester egg with a twicedated shell and a dynamight right for Pavl the Curate; a collera morbous for Mann in the Cloack; a starr and girton for Draper and Deane; for Will-of-the-Wisp and Barny-the-Bark two mangolds noble to sweeden their bitters; for Oliver Bound a way in his frey; for Seumas, thought little, a crown he feels big; a tibertine's pile with a Congoswood cross on the back for Sunny Twimjim. (James Joyce, "Anna Livia Plurabelle," *Finnegans Wake*)

The Gate to the Underworld

On the riverbank, just across the Tiber from the Mausoleum of Hadrian, there is in Piranesi's drawing a depiction of a structure enclosing a crater in the land. It is labeled *Terentus occulens aram Ditis et Proserpinae,* "the *Terentus* covering/hiding the altar of Dis and Proserpina." The Terentus was the site of the *ludi saeculares,* the "secular games," held approximately every hundred years. The site of the [GAME]s occludes a means of access to the dark void beneath it. This forms a point of connection in "The Eternal City" to a subterranean labyrinth of which the overlying city is an iteration. The en[CRYPT]ed underworld, the world beyond the real, with its sevenfold, labyrinthine geography, is the unknown that can be reached through the known, the city labyrinth above. Piranesi's crater is a Viconian keyhole, a Freudian screen.

In his flight into the unknown of the labyrinth, Piranesi displays his terror of the all-inclusivity of the known. The *Campo Marzio Ichnographia* and the *Scienza Nuova* cry out for a halt to the lowering of the rationalist cage. No order from the outside, no structural order, they plead, is necessary in a system that is, in a large sense, chaotic, but that has internal ordering threads.

A carriageable route leads you to the edge of the unknown. (André Breton, poem fragment from *The Manifesto of Surrealism*)

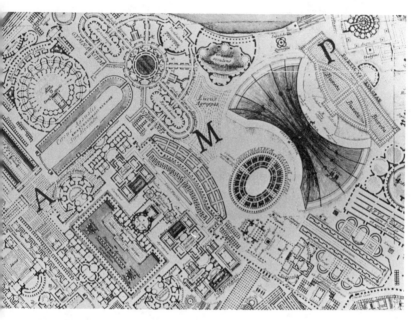

Detail from Giovanni Battista Piranesi, *Il Campo Marzio dell'Antica Roma: Ichnographia* (1762)

Theseus in the Cretan labyrinth is Ulysses in the *Odyssey* is Proserpina in the underworld. He is also Dante, who descends into hell to find Minos, the former proprietor of the Cretan labyrinth, now acting as the judge who assigns each shade his or her proper circle. Guarding the seventh circle is the "infamy of Crete," the Minotaur.

> Like Dante, Vico regarded language as the gateway to truth and "poetic wisdom" as the most essential starting point, yet a transcendental vision as a final destination. Like Dante, too, he traversed a number of circles . . . before reaching his final vision. The difference is that Vico's path did indeed circle back on itself. (Donald Kelley, "Vico's Road: From Philosophy to Jurisprudence and Back")

> And ere that again, leada, laida, all unraidy, too faint to buoy the fairiest rider, too frail to flirt with a cygnet's plume, she was licked by a hound, Chirripa-Chirruta, while poing her pee, pure and simple, on the spur of the hill in old Kippure, in birdsong and shearingtime, but first of all, worst of all, the wiggly livvly, she sideslipped out by a gap in the Devil's glen while Sally her nurse was sound asleep in a sloot and, feefee fiefie, fell over a spillway before she found her stride and lay and wriggled in all the stagnant black pools of rainy under a fallow coo and she laughed innocefree with her limbs aloft and a whole drove of maiden hawthorns blushing and looking askance upon her. (James Joyce, *Finnegans Wake*)

Theseus returns. Ulysses returns. Proserpina, hapless daughter, returns, and returns, and returns, tying the labyrinth to time as well as to space.

The Seasonal Clock

To the east of the crater in the drawing lies an enormous configuration of lines shaped like a concave lens. These denote the paths of the sun across the earth at various times of the year, forming, with the sun, a timepiece.

Piranesi's reaction of shock looks backward to prehistory in its invocation of myth and its orientation toward source and forward to modernism in its fragmentation and abstraction, and in its distant viewpoint. Like a shattered narrative, the drawing's temporal orientation is discontinuous and tends to return to familiar points by means of fragments of circles and spirals. The shattering of time figures in two ways here. The drawing both represents a shattering and operates as a shatterer. It is, like the fractured narrative of Joyce, "the future Presentation of the Past."

> Our wholemole millwheeling vicociclometer, a tetradomational gazebocroticon (the "Mamma Lujah" known to every school-boy scandaller, be he Matty, Marky, Lukey or John-a-Donk), autokinatonetically preprovided with a clappercoupling smelting-works exprogressive process, (for the farmer, his son and their homely codes, known as eggburst, eggblend, eggburial and hatch-as-hatch-can) receives through a portal vein the dialytically separated elements of precedent decomposition for the verypet-purpose of subsequent recombination so that the heroticisms, catastrophes and eccentricities transmitted by the ancient legacy of the past, type by tope, letter from litter, word at ward, with sendence of sundance, since the days of Plooney and Columcellas when Giacinta, Pervenche and Margaret swayed over the all-too-ghoulish and illyrical and innumantic in our mutter nation, all, anastomosically assimilated and preteridentified paraidiotically, in fact, the sameold gamebold adomic structure of our Finnius the old One, as highly charged with electrons as hophazards can effec-tive it, may be there for you, Cockalooralooraloomenos, when cup, platter and pot come piping hot, as sure as herself pits hen to paper and there's scribings scrawled on eggs [HATCHERY].

> Of cause, so! And in effect, as? (James Joyce, *Finne-gans Wake*)

The vicociclometer is not the tool of the geometer. Its millwheeling motion suggests a ponderous, cyclical measurement, but it is incapable of measuring the shortest distance between two points. It measures not earth but ideas, not the wall but the way. It was constructed in the *Scienza Nuova*, Piranesi mapped its movements, which are discontinuous pieces of spiral, and over its path Joyce suspended collages of words: interlacing branches heavy with glittering leaves, themselves a thing, their quivering, dappled shade another, superimposed on the always turning, fragmented path.

The universe from which our giants withdraw is the universe of the machine. The object of their desires is the universe of language, the universe of gods, heroes, and men.

> It is not in the premise that reality
> Is a solid. It may be a shade that traverses
> A dust, a force that traverses a shade.
> (Wallace Stevens, "An Ordinary Evening in New Haven")

> He married his markets, cheap by foul, I know, like any Etrurian Catholic Heathen, in their pinky limony creamy birnies and their indienne mauves. But at milkidmass who was the spouse? Then all that was was fair. Tys Elvenland! Teems of times and happy returns. The seim anew. Ordovico or viricordo. Anna was, Livia is, Plurabelle's to be. (James Joyce, "Anna Livia Plurabelle" *Finnegans Wake*)

Collision

Clinamen: A swerving.

> The clinamen is an essential concept in [Michel] Serres' interpretation of Lucretius' *De Rerum Natura*. . . . The clinamen marks the moment when an atom in laminar flow deviates from its path, collides with another atom, and initiates the formation of things and ultimately of worlds. (Editors' note to Serres' "Language and Space," *Hermes: Literature, Science, Philosophy*)

Annie Dillard writes that *Finnegans Wake* comes "close to vaporizing the world and making of language a genuine stuff" (*Living by Fiction*, 72). The book, like Piranesi's drawing, presents a world as it is imbedded in the language (verbal or architectural). Just as *Finnegans Wake* is a "lousy story" so is the *Campo Marzio* a crummy map. The material world we know is nearly vaporized in the collision that produces these collections of fragments, but the resulting new worlds comment on the world we know as insightfully, perhaps more so, as the most finely wrought mimetic object.

> We find poetic truth struck out by the collision rather than the collusion of images. (C. Day Lewis, *The Poetic Image*)

The Wandering Rocks, the walls of the labyrinth, collide and crumble to bits. The resulting chaotic configuration of fragments suggests a new enclosure, a new labyrinth, inviting and forbidding, in which the wanderer finds another way.

What has gone? How it ends?

Begin to forget it. It will remember itself from every sides, with all gestures, in each our word. Today's truth, tomorrow's trend.

Forget, remember! (James Joyce, *Finnegans Wake*)

Construction Two:
La Pianta di Ampio Magnifico Collegio

An infamous private ailment (vulgovarioveneral) had claimed endright, closed his vicious circle, snap.

James Joyce, *Finnegans Wake*, 98.18–19

Prologue: On Section (*Passagen*)

A *section* is an assemblage of dark spots on a plane.[7] It maps the residual of surgery on an object by a plane of incision. Each spot marks the instant an axis of inscription converges with an axis of incision. The sectioned object undergoes permutations in a logical system of representation— a system of coordinates. The logic of the representation resembles the logic imposed upon the physical world: the logic of gravity. Within this imposed structure, objects are ascribed an orientation with respect to the center of the planet that becomes translated into an orientation with respect to the surface of the planet. Thus, objects are endowed with tops and bottoms (the parts most distal and most proximal, respectively, to the planet's center).

On the plane of inscription, the scratchings that represent the object sliced by a plane perpendicular to the line connecting "top" and "bottom" are called the plan. A plan is a section that demands the presence of gravity. *Plan* has a concise meaning, therefore, only in a world in which the concepts of heaviness and lightness are distinct and unambiguous.

We, of course, do not live in such a positivist's paradise. The world and the language are all tangled around each other. In his astonishingly prolific life, Giambattista Piranesi produced only one building design that he called a plan: the *Pianta di ampio magnifico Collegio*. Having been accused by the *Académie de France* of being incapable of producing a proper plan, the Italian responded with the *Collegio* drawing. It looks very much like a plan:

lines on paper generated by geometry, [POCHE] indicating columns and walls, solid and dotted lines indicating stairs, vaults, and beams. It appears to be connected rather directly to the world of tension and compression—and it is connected, but insidiously. A close examination reveals that the "building" represented by this single drawing is not an enclosure of stone and wood and plaster but rather a much more intricate and difficult construction.

Piranesi's is a plan divorced from gravity, a section through an object constructed with ideas, an *ampio* (both "ample" and "diffuse") *Collegio* (a "college," an "assembly"). It is a translucent slice, a window; also a slicer—Piranesi's critical knife, cutting open, laying bare, revealing. The section (the having-been-cut) is itself an instrument of incision: it is both the plane of inscription and the plane of incision. The section makes a connection between worlds. It delineates the here and serves as an interface between theres.

So, what is here? In the gravity world we read (both in the architectural metalanguage of the plan and in Piranesi's inscription) a text composed of bits and pieces of conventional building from the Greco-Roman tradition: a critical text, commenting on baroque architecture. But what is here in the grand field? What do we read when the plan becomes only what we really have here, a network of tiny canals of engraver's ink sucked up and frozen on a sheet of paper?

Geometry. A series of concentric rings not quite contained by a square. Some geometric barnacles clinging to the periphery. The rings are sliced into eight equal pieces by a web of eight radial swaths which make gestures toward intersection at an unmarked center. We focus on this wheel, this window; the power of the instrument seems to reside here. Circles cut by V's. Eight V's in a circle.

《The strategy of criticism is located in the object of criticism. . . . It is not necessary to introduce methods to read this text: the method is in the text. The text is its own criticism, its own explication, its own application. This is not a special case: it is one that is perfectly generalizable. Why should there be dichotomy between texts, between the ones that operate and the ones that are operated upon? There are texts, and that is all.》 《Michel Serres, *Hermes,* 38》

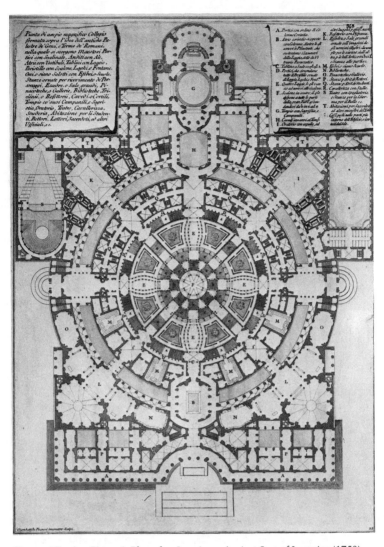

Giovanni Battista Piranesi, *Plan of an Imaginary Ancient Seat of Learning* (1750)

《Snicker-snack!》 《This "scission" . . . marks the arbitrary insertion of the letter-opener by which the reading process is opened
up indifferently here or there, the cutting edge of writing which
begins with the reading of some sequence clipped out from
there or here, the chancy but necessary repetition of the already-
thereness of some (other) text, the sharp blade of decision.》
《Lewis Carroll, "Jabberwocky"》 《Jacques Derrida, *Dissemination*, 300–301》

With two incisions in V configuration, we can remove a first piece.
Call it VARIORUM. With this V-section removed, the thing collapses into a
tangled mess, like the "lace apron" of a cat on the dissection table. But the
two incisions yield two ends. Grasp them in two hands and hold the slice up
to the light. Here are seven sections of section—read them.

[MAPPING]

Vagary
Invagination
Vessel
Void
Verge
Violation
Interval

Variorum

《[L *variorum* of various persons, . . . in the phrase *cum notis
variorum* with the notes of various persons] 1: an edition or text
esp. of a classical author with notes by different persons 2: an
edition of a publication containing variant readings of the text.》
《*Webster's Third New International Dictionary of the English
Language*》
《Aighuh—and no manes and horses' trot? butt, butt
Of earth, birds spreading harps, two manes a pair
Of birds, each bird a word, a streaming gut
Trot, trot—? No horse is here, no horse is there?
Says you! Then I—fellow me, airs! we'll make
Wood horse, and recognize it with our words—

Not it—nine less two!—as many as take
To make a dead man purple in the face,
Full dress to rise and circle thru a pace
Trained horses—in latticed orchards, (switch!) birds [GAME].》
⟪Louis Zukofsky, "A," 7:45–46⟫

Vagary

⟪1 *archaic:* JOURNEY, EXCURSION, TOUR 2 *archaic:* an aimless digression . . . 4: a departure from the expected, normal, or logical order or course.》 ⟪*Webster's Third New International Dictionary of the English Language*⟫

⟪The path of the carding wheels is straight and crooked.》 ⟪Heraclitus, Fragment LXXIV⟫

⟪On old Olympus' towering top, a Finn and German viewed . . . 》 [8]

The tenth, and longest, pair of cranial nerves is called vagus, "wandering," and it wanders from the back of the head down into the core of the belly. The word is akin to *prevaricate,* "to walk knock-kneed," with crooked feet. A person who ambulates with crooked feet leaves tracks of nonconvergent V's, bearing a resemblance to [HEN] tracks, chicken scratch, crooked T's, tap-tap-taps [HATCHERY]. She is like crooked-footed Oedipus, whose tracks formed a map of his life: two distinct lines, the line of seeking the cause of devastation and the line of being the cause of devastation, heading toward convergence [MAPPING]. Oedipus, unwitting prevaricator, walked in V-fashion and lived two lives that met in V-fashion. At the point of convergence—the focal point, the vanishing point—Oedipus jabbed out his eyes. Seeing (constructing relations among the signs) was for him the interface (a transverse section) between collection and speculation, between in-front-of-the-eyes perception and behind-the-eyes perception.

⟪V. at the age of thirty-three . . . had found love at last in her peregrinations through (let us be honest) a world if not created then at least described to its fullest by Karl Baedeker of Leipzig. This is a curious country, populated only by a breed called "tourists." Its landscape is one of inanimate monuments and buildings. . . . More than this it is two-dimensional, as is the Street, as are the pages and maps of those little red handbooks.⟫ ⟪Thomas Pynchon, *V.*, 384⟫

⟪Follow the tour guide
accurately.
When you will have reached
the place where the hotel is located (it is the best
existing hotel)
you'll see that you
have found absolutely
—go on calmly—nothing.
The tour guide does not lie [MAPPING].⟫ ⟪Giorgio Caproni, "Sure Direction," 222⟫

⟪Lens your dappled yeye here, mine's presbyoperian [POCHE].⟫ ⟪*FW*, 293.32–294.01⟫

In front of the focal point, what is seen is *poché,* black spots on the eye. Resident poché we call floaters: bits of detritus floating passively in the vitreous humor, like plankton (the "wandering ones"). Alien poché—Piranesi's drawing, a collection of black spots—held in front of the eye describes a screen or window through which to see.

The section is an eye through which the eye sees. The transmission of information begins at the point of a V, or at the intersection of V's, at the back of the eye. The section, the poché, is in front of the eye, in the eye, at the back of the eye. Behind the eye, it can remain intact (an object seen); it can become a center (an object analyzed); or it can become disseminated (an object, a thrown-in-the-way, cut apart into bits that drift and explore—inquire, seek, ramify, connecting to other bits, forming a new text in which shards of the old object are embedded).

⟪"It is this way with sewer stories. They just are. Truth or falsity don't apply."⟫ ⟪Thomas Pynchon, *V.,* 108⟫

Invagination

⟪The way up and down is one and the same.⟫ ⟪Heraclitus, Fragment CIII⟫

⟪In the world of eternal return the weight of unbearable responsibility lies heavy on every move we make. That is why Nietzsche called the idea of eternal return the heaviest of burdens (*das schwerste Gewicht*).

If eternal return is the heaviest of burdens, then our lives can stand out against it in all their splendid lightness. But is heaviness truly deplorable and lightness splendid?

The heaviest of burdens crushes us, we sink beneath it, it pins us to the ground. But in the love poetry of every age, the woman longs to be weighed down by the man's body.[9] The heaviest of burdens is therefore simultaneously an image of life's most intense fulfillment. The heavier the burden, the closer our lives come to the earth, the more real and truthful they become.

Conversely, the absolute absence of a burden causes man to be lighter than air, to soar into the heights, take leave of the earth and his earthly being, and become only half real, his movements as free as they are insignificant.

What then shall we choose? Weight or lightness?》
《Milan Kundera, *The Unbearable Lightness of Being, 5*》

We perceive both space and time, telescopically, in V's. At the point of the V, at the vanishing point, is a connection—perhaps theological, perhaps theosophical, perhaps temporal, perhaps spatial. It is a connection between worlds: an omphalos, a Brennschluss point, a vertex. The *Collegio* drawing forms a section through such a connection. It is a model of an excluded middle. It is the place where concepts we call opposing flow into one another, a critical point of ambiguity, the site of "both/and."

《I wonder if I shall fall right through the earth! How funny it'll seem to come out among the people that walk with their heads downwards! The antipathies, I think—.》 《Lewis Carroll, *Alice's Adventures in Wonderland, 19*》

If we step back for a moment into the world of the drawing as a representation of building, we can read Piranesi's clue. Enter this building through one of its portals. Proceed down the undulating, notched axis before you. As you approach the terminus of the axis, you find not a great center-marking rotunda, but an enormous tangle of stairs that carry you right-left-up-down and send you suddenly moving down one of the other seven axes, into the labyrinth of the building. Inevitably, your wanderings will bring you to another axis that will again draw you toward that centerless middle that flings you out again. The equivocal center does not perform its traditional duty of stabilizing the structure. It is an eccentric center. The building is like Varvara Stepanova's set for *Tarelkin's Death*: the terrible interrogation machine, sucking in, whirling around, expelling, surrounded by a collection of collapsing and self-reassembling chairs and exploding tables.

《Let's pretend the glass has got soft like gauze, so that we can
get through. Why, it's turning into a sort of mist now, I declare!》
《Lewis Carroll, *Through the Looking Glass*, 129》

It is the site of "both/and," the locus of "extravent intervulve coupling," a doubling, "one world burrowing on another" (*FW*, 314.20; 275.5). Worlds within worlds, tubes within tubes. Connected are square and circle, male and female, rational and irrational, implosion and explosion. Sucking in, whirling around, and expelling: digestion, respiration, reproduction, creative thought. It is a section through a body, a universe, a book.

A spherical cell is violated by a line-driven cell. The tail (the line) breaks off. Information flows. The construction begins. The cell-within-a-cell splits and doubles: one into two into four into eight. Now it is a round, bumpy cluster of cells with a void inside. Blastopore [ROCKET]! The outer wall collapses inward at a tiny point. Over the lip of this imploding hole slide streaky layers of differentiated cells—endoderm, mesoderm, notochord. The outside becomes the inside. Gastrulation: invagination, involution, epiboly. Implosion. How we achieve our tube-within-a-tubeness.

We are tubes within tubes (continuous outer-inner surfaces) with intricately articulated interstices—ampio. Systems of cells are woven into a dense textile, filling the spaces between inside and outside surface: hierarchies from bone-muscle-nerve-blood vessel to C HOPKINS CaFe, Mighty good, Naturally Clean [10] to quarks and leptons. A section will reveal that the body, the container, is an architecture in the interval.

《He indeed was visited by dreams in which he had shrunk to
sub-microscopic size and entered a brain, strolling in through
some forehead's pore and into the cul-de-sac of a sweat gland.
Struggling out of a jungle of capillaries, there he would finally
reach bone; down then through the skull, dura mater, arachnoid,
pia mater to the fissure floored sea of cerebrospinal fluid. And
there he would float before final assault on the gray hemispheres:
the soul.

Nodes of Ranvier, sheath of Schwann, vein of Galen;
tiny Stencil wandered all night long among the silent immense
lightning bursts of nerve-impulses crossing a synapse; the waving
dendrites, the nerve autobahns chaining away to God knew where
in receding clusters of end-bulbs. A stranger in this landscape, it
never occurred to him to ask whose brain he was in. Perhaps his
own.》《Thomas Pynchon, *V.*, 443》[11]

《The Lord whose oracle is in Delphi neither declares nor conceals,
but gives a sign.》《Heraclitus, Fragment XXXIII》

Vessel

A [VESSEL] is both a container and a conduit, the sea and the
ship. It is the thing disseminated and the instrument of dissemination. Vessels are instruments of flux: through them flow information, oxygen, food, antibodies, semen. The drawing may be read as a *vas deferens,* a deferent[12] vessel: a vessel of difference and deference, a vas différance. Standing in for an artificial erection (like Isis' artifice—the other of Daedalus' artifice), it marks the point of exchange, the lip, the rim of the flow. The verge, the place where something is about to happen.

《But in the dynamic space of the living [ROCKET], the double
integral has a different meaning. To integrate here is to operate on
a rate of exchange so that time falls away: change is stilled. . . .
"Meters per second" will integrate to "meters." The moving
vehicle is frozen, in space, to become architecture, and timeless.
It was never launched. It will never fall.》《Thomas Pynchon,
Gravity's Rainbow, 350》

The *rochetto* is a woman's tool, an instrument of textile-making.
The erection at Cape Canaveral meets Isis' construction, a woman's tool, at
the site of drawing, perhaps not too surprised at the [MIRROR] image it
encounters.

《Construct ann aquilittoral dryankle Probe loom! [WEAVING]
With his primal handstoe in his sole salivarium. Concoct an
equo-angular trilitter. (As Rhombulus and Rhebus went building
rhomes one day.)》《*FW,* 286.19–22》

Here is the vesica piscis, fish bladder, vessel of flux, where male and female, space and time, science and magic meet. It is a section through *Finnegans Wake* or through the cosmos. Follow Joyce's instructions for perceiving it three-dimensionally: extruding Euclid across the border into the non-Euclidean world, cut a transverse section through that, and you will have Piranesi's construction.

《Show that the median, hce che ech, intersecting at royde angles the parilegs of a given obtuse one biscuts the arcs that are in curveachord behind. Brickbaths. The family umbroglia.》《Till its nether nadir is vortically where (allow me aright to two cute winkles) its naval's napex will have to beandbe.》《*FW*, 283.32– 284.4; 297.12–14》

The [HEN]'s [LETTER] of *Finnegans Wake,* the disseminated, signifying creation—the act of copulation and the act of city-building—is the [POCHE] of the [VESSEL]. The letter is *thalatta* (*thalassa*) is the ladder— Jacob's or Wittgenstein's, the sea and the conduit. The letter is poché, black spots scattered, and also systems of T's, trabeation, architecture.

《The hidden attunement is better than the obvious one.》《Heraclitus, Fragment LXXX》

《Peep inside the cerebralised saucepan of this eer illwinded goodfornobody you would see in his house of thoughtsam (was you, that is, decontaminated enough to look discarnate) what a jetsam litterage of convolvuli of times lost or strayed, of lands derelict and of tongues laggin too, longa yamsayore, not only that but, search lighting, beached, bashed and beaushelled *à la Mer* pharahead into faturity, your own convolvulis pickninnig capman would real to jazztfancy the novo takin place of what stale words whilom were woven with and fitted fairly featly for, so; and equally so, the crame of the whole faustian fustian, whether our launer's lightsome or your soulard's schwearmood, it is that, whenas the swiftshut scareyss of your pupilteachertaut duplex will hark back to lark to you symibellically, that, though a day be as dense as a decade, no mouth has the might to set a mearbound to the march of a landsmaul, in half a sylb, helf a solb, holf a salb onward the beast of boredom, common sense, lurking gyrographically down inside his loose Eating S.S. collar is gogoing of whisth to you sternly how—Plutonic loveliaks twintt Platonic yearlings—you must, how, in undivided reawlity draw the line somewhawre.》《*FW*, 292.13–32》

《The sea is the purest and foulest water: for fish drinkable and life-sustaining; for men undrinkable and deadly [PHARMA-KON].》《Heraclitus, Fragment LXX》

Void

The *Collegio* is a circle inscribed in a square. The square is only implied by four corners, four broken isosceles right triangles, four wide V's. The square, the created figure, is tacked to the circle, the creator figure, through the empty center, the last of the concentric rings. The omphalos supplements the phallus. The parts of Leonardo's cosmos shift and slide, now aligned on a hole, "the no placelike no timelike absolent" (*FW*, 609.2).

《Can proximity cause vertigo?

It can. When the north pole comes so close as to touch the south pole, the earth disappears and man finds himself in a void that makes his head spin and beckons him to fall.》《Milan Kundera, *Unbearable Lightness of Being*, 244》

The V's of the drawing point toward convergence, but do not converge. The vanishing point is indicated, but is not "on the map." The world of the artists Kasimir Malevich (the four-dimensional world reached by passing through the vanishing point) may be beyond this hole. The void is the passage between worlds of n and $n + 1$ dimensions. The section is a window; the void is a door.

《You can just see a little peep [UNDESIRABLE BEASTS] of the passage in Looking-Glass House, if you leave the door of our drawing-room wide open: and it's very like our passage as far as you can see, only you know it may be quite different on beyond.》《Lewis Carroll, *Through the Looking Glass*, 129》

The (strangely) looping stairs define the empty center. It is not hard to see a connection between this drawing and the centerless infinite looping of some of Piranesi's *Carceri*. "Behind these halls with their barred bulls-eyes, we suspect there are other halls just like them, deduced or deducible in every direction. The frail catwalks, the drawbridges in mid-air which almost everywhere double the galleries and the stone staircases, seem to correspond to the same desire to hurl into space all possible curves and parallels. This world closed over itself is mathematically infinite" (Yourcenar, *Dark Brain of Piranesi*, 114).

The endless repetitive climbing required in the *Collegio* center-approaching resembles the Castle-approaching of Kafka's land surveyor; which, as Borges has pointed out, is like the Tortoise-approaching of Achilles; which, as Douglas Hofstadter has pointed out, is like the activity of those who populate the drawings of M. C. Escher; which is something like the stair-climbing of Kerensky in Eisenstein's *October*, a montage sequence inspired by the *Carceri*.

《Flop! Your rere gait's creakorheuman bitts your butts disagrees.》 《*FW*, 214.21–22》

《Holy-Center-Approaching[, a] 《pastime [with] about the same vulnerability to record-breakers as baseball, a sport also well-spidered with white suggestions of the sinister[,]》 is soon to be the number one Zonal pastime.》 《Thomas Pynchon, *Gravity's Rainbow*, 592, 593, 592》

To score, to reach the center, is to make the leap, to traverse the passage between worlds, to fall down the hole, to climb Jacob's ladder: to come to an end that is a beginning. The most powerful, sublime passages are those for which the other side is unknown or unspeakable, in which the void is the middle between known and unknown, between speakable and unspeakable. Wittgenstein's *Tractatus*-closing aphorism ("what we cannot speak about we must pass over in silence") is a section—a middle—delineating the border between the unspeakable and language. It is what language cannot describe described with language. It points out the difficulty of middles, places where emptiness and intricacy are the same, places of perplexing (thoroughly woven) emptiness. The void where the family secrets are en[CRYPT]ted—the "family umbroglia."

The (void) center does not hold, but the word is used to describe the condition. So the center both holds and does not hold. It is in a holding pattern.

《In the buginning is the woid, in the muddle is the sound-dance

and thereinofter you're in the unbewised again, vund vulsyvolsy.》
《*FW*, 378.29–31》

《It is here you must look, at the center of our galaxy, where all
calculations and instruments point to the presence of an enormous bodily mass which however cannot be seen. Spider webs of
radiation and gas, perhaps left entangled at the time of the last ex-
plosions, prove that in their midst lies one of these so-called holes,
now spent like an old crater. All that surrounds us, the wheel of
planetary systems and constellations and branches of the milky
way, every single thing in our galaxy is pivoted on this implosion
plunged inside itself. That is my pole, my [MIRROR], my secret
homeland.》《Italo Calvino, "The Implosion," 221》

Verge

《[me, fr. L. *Virga* twig, rod, streak, stripe—more at whisk] 1a (1):
a rod or staff carried as an emblem of authority or as a symbol
of office . . . b (1): the spindle of a watch balance; esp: a spindle
with pallets in an old vertical escapement c: the male intromittent
organ of any of various invertebrates . . . d (2): a bobbin guide on
a lace machine 2a: something that borders, limits, or bounds . . .
(2) obs: an enclosing band: *circlet, ring* . . . also: rim, brim . . .
(7) *horizon* . . . (8): the edge of the tiling projecting over the gable
of a roof . . . b: the point marking the beginning of a new or different state, condition, or action: brink, *threshold.*》《*Webster's
Third New International Dictionary of the English Language*》

《Immortals are mortal, mortals immortal, living the others' death,
dead in the others' life.》《Heraclitus, Fragment XCII》

《[The equations predicting black holes] have not one but two
solutions. In the second solution, the equations yield a "white
hole," a center from which energy and matter radiate outward
rather than being sucked in as they are in a black hole. . . . [A]
black hole can be transformed into a white hole by reversing the
value of time in the equations. . . . If the substance of the uni-

《verse is being sucked into black holes, it is being spewed out again from white holes in a circular dialectic in which annihilation and rebirth are simply two sides of the same coin.》 《N. Katherine Hayles, *Cosmic Web*, 195–196》

《Rachel was looking into the [MIRROR] at an angle of 45 [degrees], and so had a view of the face [of a clock] turned toward the room and the face on the other side, reflected in the mirror; here were time and reverse-time, co-existing, cancelling one another exactly out.》 《Skeletons, carapaces, no matter: her inside too was her outside.》 《Thomas Pynchon, *V.*, 36; 426》

《Consider coal and steel. There is a place where they meet. The interface between coal and steel is coal tar. Imagine coal, down in the earth, dead black, no light, the very substance of death. Death ancient, prehistoric, species *we will never see again*. Growing older, blacker, deeper, in layers of perpetual night. Above ground, the steel rolls out fiery, bright. But to make steel the coal tars, darker and heavier, must be taken from the original coal. Earth's excrement, purged out for the ennoblement of shining steel.》 《Thomas Pynchon, *Gravity's Rainbow*, 194》

Violation

《Behind all European faiths, religious and political, we find the first chapter of Genesis, which tells us that the world was created properly [THE PROPER], that human existence is good, and that we are therefore entitled to multiply. Let us call this basic faith a *categorical agreement with being*. . . . The aesthetic ideal of the categorical agreement with being is a world in which shit is denied and everyone acts as though it did not exist. This aesthetic ideal [the result of Hegel's wiping] is called kitsch.》 《Milan Kundera, *Unbearable Lightness of Being*, 248》

Piranesi's architecture is contaminated. It is kitsch (if one will allow the anachronism) violated by bits of detritus, bits of digested and undigested material [HOUSE, VESSEL].[13] It is a metacommentary on the paradox of kitsch: kitsch is centered around an absence. This center is unspeakable

and unapproachable because it (the tube within a tube) is a vessel of—
what else?—excrement, a violation of the ideal. In persistent avoidance
(a-voidance) of shit, shit becomes the focus, the center. Rupture—void—
the center; and it "hits the fan," is disseminated, making a dappled thing,
mottled, motley, dark-spotted, ampio. A [ROCKET] is propelled this way,
by the expulsion of its own waste.

⟪Imagine that you have swallowed a cylindrical [MIRROR].
Upright, bigger than you are. . . . This glass column traverses,
dominates, regulates, and reflects, in its numerous polysemy, the
entire set of squares.

It is a Tower of [BABEL] in which multiple languages
and forms of writing bump into each other or mingle with each
other, constantly being transformed and engendered through their
most unreconcilable otherness to each other, an otherness which
is strongly affirmed, too, for plurality here is bottomless and is not
lived as negativity, with any nostalgia for lost unity.⟫ ⟪Jacques
Derrida, *Dissemination,* 341⟫

In a film that was originally and significantly called *Edge City* (re-
released as *Repo Man*), there is a character called Miller, a repo-lot watch-
dog, man of garbage, who rides buses over rhizomatous pathways. Miller is
an advocate of Dioretix, a mind-over-matter pop movement which, like its
homophonic counterpart, voids weight, producing lightness. The hot car, in
Miller's hands, becomes a virtual rocket.

⟪The question: to explode or to implode, would it again come
up? Absorbed by the vortex of this galaxy, would one reappear in
other times and other skies? To sink here into profound silence, to
express oneself there in flaming shrieks of another language? To
absorb here evil and good like a sponge in the shade, to gush out
there like a dazzling jet, to spread, expend, lose oneself?⟫ ⟪Italo
Calvino, "The Implosion," 215⟫

⟪Even in Florence . . . he had noted an obsession with bodily in-
corporating little bits of inert matter.⟫ ⟪Flip!⟫ ⟪Thomas Pynchon,
V., 459⟫ ⟪*FW,* 213.22⟫

We cannot see V-particles, but we know they have been there, tiny
collision bits leaving little V-shaped tracks. The angles of history.

《The fairest order in the world is a heap of random sweepings.》
《Heraclitus, Fragment CXXV》

[INTERVAL]
《Flep!》 《*FW*, 213.23》

Interval results from the coupling of *inter* ("between, among") and *vallum* ("palisade or wall," from *vallus*, "post or stake"). (This suggests that an architecture of the interval is both among the walls and among—in the interstices between—the posts, or poles, totem or otherwise.) *Interval,* then, literally means "between the walls," suggesting a place that might be occupied, a space. It elicits a number of images. One is the place between or among the walls of a labyrinth—the place of wandering, of seeking, of exploratory movement that might be mapped.

Maps themselves exist in intervals. They are not what they purport to be. True, they represent places—geography—but, equally important, they concern time—chronology—what we do, how we move through our lives. Maps, then, exist in the interval between geography and chronology. They exist in the interval between reality and the ordered experience of it [MAPPING].

The schema of a map's generation (that experience of reality) is embedded in the map itself. This suggests a second image of interval: the place within the wall of an object in which lie the tools of that object's generation. This object, then, contains the schema, or tools, with which it was made. It is like the Ideal Palace of Cheval or Carlo Scarpa's Abatellis Palace in Palermo, for which working drawings were made on the walls themselves, then covered over with plaster (see Frascari, "Carlo Scarpa," 9).

A third image is the gap between boundaries, the place where the edges of things come close to touching. The place of architecture seems to be here (as well as in its conventional disciplinary capsule that rather sheepishly embeds itself in an imagined wall between art and science). This architecture is not disciplinary, but interdisciplinary. It seeps out of its capsule and bleeds into the interstices, the intervals among the dissolving walls of other capsules: philosophy, science, literature. Architecture not in a capsule, but in a soup.[14]

《Stencil sketched the entire history of V. that night and strengthened a long suspicion. That it did add up only to the recurrence of an initial and a few dead objects.》《Thomas Pynchon, *V.,* 419》

《Graspings: wholes and not wholes, convergent and divergent, consonant dissonant, from all things one and from one thing all.》《Heraclitus, Fragment CXXIV》[15]

《Light wave and quantum, we have good proof both exist:
Our present effort is to see how this is: to
Perfect the composition of a two-point view

. . . .

Build it.》《Louis Zukofsky, "*A,*" 8:55–56》

Postscrypt: Taupologie of the *Collegio*

The ghosts of many fathers will be conjured, but with the caveat that this postscrypt demands that we be aware of an inter[WEAVING] of speech and writing, muddying the distinction between the visual and the verbal. These fathers will not be named—yet.

A Beginning

Taupologie is homophonous with and similar to, yet different from, topology. *Taupologie* is the name of the activity of *la taupe,* "the mole," a small, soft creature with hidden ears who doesn't see very well and who tunnels about in the dark.[16] *Webster's* gives us other definitions of *mole:* a congenital ("marking a beginning") dark spot on a surface; one who works in the dark; a massive work formed of masonry and large [STONE]s or earth laid in the sea (*la mer[e]*) as a pier or breakwater; an abnormal mass in the uterus, especially when containing fetal tissues (marking a beginning); a gram molecule (a little bit of something). This constellation of structures about a four-letter word typifies the activity of the webster, who is concerned with the activity of webmaking. One concerned with the activity of the mole, who operates in dark soil, will be called a mole-ster. The activity of the mole-ster is connected to topology, which has to do with holes and ruptures in things.

Another Beginning

The formidable ghost of Walter Benjamin, with his text on *Origin* in hand, has already been conjured. In what he called in that text a children's nursery (that messy cacaphonous place), we might hear a nursery rhyme:

Here's the tale of Michael Finnegan.

He grew whiskers on his chinnegan.

He grew fat and then grew thin again.

Poor old Michael Finnegan. Begin again.

(And so on . . .)

Michael Finnegan resembles the bearded father in an illustration from the *Chymica Vannus dell'Alchimia, o la scienza sognata*. In that picture, a father/king is on the verge of devouring his son—a representation of primary material devouring and spewing itself back out, growing fat and thin again in a neverending cycle. This calls to mind another Finnegan and a whole slew of fathers, the giant a-gents of history, dying and waking, rising and falling, growing fat and thin, all asking the question, "Which came first, the chicken or the egg?" James Joyce's text bears the influence of the strong poetic wisdom of Giambattista Vico, father of both Joyce and Piranesi.

Edward Said (in *Beginnings*) wrote: "[Vico] is the first philosopher of beginnings, not because he was the first in time to think as he did . . . but because for him a beginning is at once never given and always indefinite or divined and yet always asserted at considerable expense" (350). Vico's beginning is a Joycean "begidding"—a begetting of giddy beginnings—a biting of the apple. Vico's world "begins among stones, rocks, frogs, and cicadas, rather like Yeats' 'foul rag-and-bone shop of the heart.' This is quite another world from Plato's realm of forms or from Descartes' clear and distinct ideas" (348). It is like the "children's nursery" or Joyce's House O'Shea or O'Shame, with its

> warped flooring . . . persianly literatured with burst loveletters,
> telltale stories, stickyback snaps, doubtful eggshells, bouchers,
> flints, borers, puffers, amygdaloid almonds, rindless raisins,
> alphybettyformed verbage, vivlical viasses, ompiter dictas, visus
> umbique, ahems and ahahs, imeffible tries at speech unasylla-
> bled, you owe mes, eyoldhyms, fluefoul smut, fallen lucifers,
> vestas which had served, showered ornaments, borrowed brogues,
> reversibles jackets, blackeye lenses, family jars [VESSEL], false-
> hair shirts, Godforsaken scapulars, neverworn breeches, cutthroat
> ties, counterfeit franks, best intentions, curried notes, upset latten
> tintacks, unused mill and stumpling stones, twisted quills, painful
> digests, magnifying wineglasses, solid objects cast at goblins, once

current puns, quashed quotatoes, messes of mottage, unquestionable issue papers, seedy ejaculations (*FW*, 183.8–23),

and no doubt the gargantuan ghost of Rabelais dancing diabolically in the
rubble.

Vico recognized no distinction between theory and practice. In his
text are braided together speculations on the cycles of history and descriptions of (to paraphrase and parody Said) the primitive mothers copulating
with their men in caves. (Please to note, copulating, like moles, in caves not
in primitive huts, which effectively killed this activity.)

The primitive hut is the [HOUSE] of my fathers. But there is, here,
the beginning of an intrusive presence in this house [HATCHERY]:

> She transforms, she acts: the old culture will soon be the new. She
> is mixed up in dirty things; she has no cleanliness phobia—the
> proper housecleaning attacks that hysterics sometimes suffer. She
> handles filth, manipulates wastes, buries placentas, and burns the
> cauls of newborn babies for luck. She makes partial objects useful,
> puts them back in circulation properly [THE PROPER]. What a
> fine mess! (Cixous and Clément, *Newly Born Woman*, 36)[17]

To make partial objects circulate . . . At about the same time that the Abbaye
("the Father") Laugier is drawing the line of rationality between the primitive
hut and the immutable laws of architecture, creating a literally phallocentric architecture, there is, just to the south and east, a delirious operative at
work, scratching dark spots on a surface, making a massive work of masonry
and large stones, like a Cyclops—who doesn't see very well—making an
abnormal mass. A "dark-brained"[18] individual incises the canals that make
an eight-legged critter [UNDESIRABLE BEASTS], an ample, diffuse, and
magnificent assemblage, the work of a mole-ster.

This work is Piranesi's *Pianta di ampio magnifico Collegio,* an
image of what might be were a slice taken through a nonexistent, nonsyn-
thesized building. It is an "organism that *pretend*[s] to have a centrality but
that never achieve[s] one" (Tafuri, *Sphere and Labyrinth*, 27). What throws
us is the center, where we expect a great signifying void, the logic of the
rotunda. It throws us quite literally, shuttling us back out into the periphery
of the building via a subversive apparatus of stairs that push at the limits of
building sense and throw the logic of the rest into question and into motion.
The *Collegio* is an assemblage of [CRYPT]s, glands, and follicles, [VESSEL]s

and valves, accommodating, checking, and diverting endless flow; a generative section that will not be extruded, will not obey the tyranny of linear time; mole-work bearing the trace of the *tarantella,* the activity of hysterics at the mercy of their motile voids.[19] A mercurial vessel. A taupologie machine: a "wholemole millwheeling vicociclometer" that "secretly undermines the laws to which it pretends to subject itself" (*Sphere and Labyrinth,* 31). A [HYSTERICAL DOCUMENT], it is a representation of the "psychical house" that Freud built, a [HOUSE] with a strange apparatus in the middle: an intricate void, where the (family) history is en[CRYPT]ed (inscribed and secreted). "A cataleptic mithyphallic! Was this *Totem Fulcrum Est* Ancestor yu hald in *Dies Eirae* where no spider webbeth?" (*FW,* 482.4–5).[20] Held-In Desire, Halled-In Desire. The *Collegio* is a paradox: a vital vivisection of a vessel of the patriarchal symbolic order dancing off the poisons of that order that circulate through its body, it is a momentary catalepsy of an architecture of desire.

At this point, the signifier "mole-ster" secretly appropriates (secretes) a third syllable, invades the void. The daughter, who is excluded from the house of "history, locked up tight between father and son" (Cixous and Clément, *Newly Born Woman,* 56), "annoys," "disturbs," and "makes indecent advances" (*molests*). The mole-ster tunnels back around in a topological move, like a Klein worm, and becomes the molester. She is *wicked:* "morally bad," "vicious," "disgustingly unpleasant."

The "Wicked Architect" attempts "to close up the distance between the written act and the committed act," to bridge the "void which cannot be represented," the place where "the drawing always stops," the space between the drawing and the construction—the [HOUSE]—with intricate, intersecting interstices (Tafuri, "'Wicked Architect," *Sphere and Labyrinth,* 47; Rossi, *Scientific Autobiography,* 24). That place forms a network of genealogical lines. "History as a 'project of crisis,' then" (Tafuri, "Historical Project," *Sphere and Labyrinth,* 13). "[Hystery] is not that which cloaks itself in indisputable 'philological proofs,' but that which recognizes itself as an 'unsafe building'" (12).

O mio padre, writing "delirious constructions" yourself, can I bite you "senza fare il passo piu lungo della gamba"—"without making a step longer than my leg," falling into the void? *La tarantola* is restless.[21]

"Mes pères, je vous lis difficilement." ("Je vous lit difficilement.") I misread you. I miswrite you. I molest you.

Another Beginning

Julia Kristeva has written: "As capitalist society is being economically and politically choked to death, discourse is wearing thin and heading for collapse at a more rapid rate than ever before. . . . Only one language grows more and more contemporary: the equivalent . . . of the language of *Finnegans Wake*" (*Desire in Language*, 92). *Finnegans Wake* is a map for an architecture of desire, in which "desire causes the signifier to appear as heterogeneous and, inversely, indicates heterogeneity through and across the signifier" (116). The *Collegio* represents an architecture of floating signifiers, an architecture that "sanction[s] the definitive divorce of architectural signs from their signifieds" (Tafuri, *Sphere and Labyrinth*, 40).

If we make a reentry into the *Collegio* through one of its grand portals, clearly inscribed in accordance with the immutable symbolic order of architectural drawings, we will get the picture, the image, but the apparatus will elude. It is far more "joyceful"[22] to enter this text by sliding in along the path of the inscribing or incising tool, sliding through a tear in the old curtains in the back of the theater (be it the magic theater or the operating theater, the domain of the magician or the surgeon), and then circulating, molelike, within the dark areas.

Construction Three: *Le Carceri*

There is a distinctive joint in *Finnegans Wake* that occurs in the final pages.[23] This joint connects the preceding six hundred and thirteen pages, which contain many references to a something known variously as the [LETTER], the litter, the ladder, and *thalatta,* among other things, to an epistle occupying five pages of text addressed to a "Reverend" and signed by "ALP," Anna Livia Plurabelle, the feminine character of the *Wake*. The joint of text comprises pages 614.27 to 615.11 ("Our wholemole millwheeling vicociclometer. . . . Of cause, so! And in effect, as?") and appears in construction 1 of this chapter.

Then begins the letter, which has been broken up and disseminated both metaphorically and literally throughout *Finnegans Wake,* and which leads to the final pages, revealing the text as an enormous circle. The vicociclometer is a flux machine—diverting flows of language and history. A machine measuring the cycle of Vico, a circle machine. A circle instrument.

Let us consider for a moment a pair of compasses. In the final pages of an article by Robin Evans called "Translations from Drawing to Building," there appear two images in which this instrument figures. One is the familiar *Ancient of Days* by William Blake, which depicts a venerable male God figure, nude, kneeling in the light plotting the universe, with widespread compasses in his left hand. In the other, a seventeenth-century painting by Giacinto Brandi, a young woman in contemporary dress, holds in her right hand, masked by shadow, a pair of nearly closed compasses, business ends pointed skywards. The painting bears the title *L'Architettura (?)*. It is worth noting that the appellation designates the woman as figurative of the discipline, not as a practitioner of it. Evans writes:

> This is one of my ambitions: the history of Blake's architect-geometer has been written a hundred times; I would like to write the history of Giacinto Brandi's, not, I hasten to add, because she is so young and pretty, but because of the uncharacteristic expression normally reserved in seventeenth-century painting for prostitutes and courtesans. The picture's subject is uncertain, its title a modern supposition resting on the fact that she holds dividers, nothing more. One might ask what such a figure is expected to do with the instrument she shows us. (16)

What, indeed?

In the hand of Blake's architect, the pair of compasses describes geometry, measures, and bisects lines and angles. It is an instrument of *emplotment*. In the hand of Brandi's allegorical shadow person, the purpose of the tool is ambiguous. Held in the position and with the delicacy of gesture of a sewing needle, it is perhaps an instrument of penetration, of puncturing. Or is it a tool for marking, tapping, making little black spots on surfaces [POCHE]? It is an instrument of *dissemination*.

The instrumentality of architectural drawing suggests that architecture "wants to be" a dissemination upon an emplotment. Conceptually, this is an absurd hybrid, or crossing (as architecture itself perhaps is), being a superimposition of a Derridean deconstructive apparatus derived from Joyce upon a concept of Paul Ricoeur's regarding the construction of historical time. (In volume 1 of *Time and Narrative*, Ricoeur suggests that in the construction of historical time a mediated relation exists between our narrative understanding, the construction of history as explanation [like the achronological historical structures of the Annales School], and the epistemologically positivistic structures of Anglo-American analytic philosophy.) For Ricoeur, the notion of emplotment—a kind of overlapping of chronological and achronological structures—forms the mediating connection, or joint. *Dissemination* is only used, never explained, by Derrida, but, as with other Derridean "concepts," the word itself points to the directions of its use, scattering small bits or seeds, and to its connection to insemination—penetrating, puncturing, and marking a surface with little black spots. Tip Tap.

Once upon a time, I was horrified to receive a request to participate in a seminar on James Joyce in which the participants were asked to select a passage from *Ulysses* and make a short response to it. My horror stemmed not from that quite appealing task, but from the identities of the other participants: the late Richard Ellmann, Joyce's biographer, and Jacques Derrida, Joyce reincarnated. In the face of this, I brandished (with delicacy of gesture) the aforementioned instrument of my profession and, in retreat, drew upon (marked upon) Joyce's text from the "architecture" section of *Ulysses*.[24]

Ulysses is constructed upon a matrix-like emplotment armature of allusions, notably to the episodes of Homer's *Odyssey*, to times of day, and to various elements of culture, colors, parts of the body, and literary techniques. *Ulysses* itself, from which, it is said, the city of Dublin could be reconstructed, is a labyrinthine composition, like a map or an architectural drawing, virtually two-dimensional. The section to which I chose to respond came from the sector called "The Lestrygonians," and referred to the episode in the *Odyssey* in which Odysseus' men were eaten while visiting the Isle of Lestrygonia. "The Lestrygonians" takes place at the lunch hour—the time of eating. It is figured by the esophagus, and the cultural element that rules it is architecture.[25] The section lies near the end of the episode, as Leopold Bloom approaches the library:

> A blind stripling stood tapping the curbstone with his slender
> cane. No tram in sight. Wants to cross.
>
> —Do you want to cross? Mr Bloom asked.
>
> The blind stripling did not answer. His wall face
> frowned weakly. He moved his head uncertainly.
>
> —You're in Dawson street, Mr Bloom said. Moles-

worth street is opposite. Do you want to cross? There's nothing in the way.

The cane moved out trembling to the left. . . .

He touched the thin elbow gently: then took the limp seeing hand to guide it forward. . . .

—Right now? First turn to the left.

The blind stripling tapped the curbstone and went on his way, drawing his cane back feeling again.

Mr Bloom walked behind the eyeless feet, a flatcut suit of herringbone tweed. Poor young fellow! How on earth did he know that van was there? Must have felt it. See things in their foreheads perhaps. Kind of sense of volume. Weight. Would he feel it if something was removed? Feel a gap. Queer idea of Dublin he must have, tapping his way round by the stones. Could he walk in a beeline if he hadn't that cane? Bloodless pious face like a fellow going in to be a priest.

Penrose! That was that chap's name. . . .

Sense of smell must be stronger too. . . . Tastes. They say you can't taste wines with your eyes shut or a cold in the head. Also smoke in the dark they say get no pleasure.

And with a woman, for instance. More shameless not seeing. That girl passing the Stewart institution, head in the air. Look at me. I have them all on. Must be strange not to see her. Kind of a form in his mind's eye. The voice temperature when he touches her with fingers must almost see the lines, the curves. His hands on her hair, for instance. Say it was black for instance. Good. We call it black. Then passing over her white skin. Different feel perhaps. Feeling of white. . . .

With a gentle finger he felt ever so slowly the hair combed back above his ears. Again. Fibres of fine fine straw. Then gently his finger felt the skin of his right cheek. Downy hair there too. Not smooth enough. The belly is the smoothest. No-one about. There he goes into Frederick street. Perhaps to Levenston's dancing academy piano. Might be settling my braces.

Walking by Doran's public house he slid his hand between waistcoat and trousers and, pulling aside his shirt gently, felt a slack fold of his belly. But I know it's whiteyellow. Want to try in the dark to see.

Poor fellow! Quite a boy. Terrible. Really terrible. What dreams would he have, not seeing? Life a dream for him. Where is the justice being born that way? All those women and children excursion beanfeast burned and drowned in New York. Holocaust. Karma they call the transmigration for sins you did in a past life the reincarnation met him pike-hoses. Dear, dear, dear. (180–182)

My response is in three parts: tap, tap, tap.

Body

The architect was, in ancient times, one who weaves, one who fabricates, in bow-and-arrow fashion.[26] So the word *architect* contains an instrument of ambiguous purpose. The bow and arrow is an instrument of love (in the hands of Cupid), and it is also an instrument of death. So it is with the architectural project.

Of the handful of architects making both material and verbal constructions of substance today, two, Bernard Tschumi and Aldo Rossi, have likened the architectural act or project to a love affair or a crime (a murder). If we look to the fabrications of the archetypal architect, we can see architecture as an instrument of love and death.

We know Daedalus as the clever inventor of many things, including the *kathetos,* or plumb line, an instrument for marking a straight line—a beeline—along the surface-to-center axis of Earth. (Daedalus was also the inventor of the compass joint, which, in its origins, was the pelvic joint of the walking—wandering—*daidalons.*[27] The compass bears the trace of vagueness.) We also know Daedalus best perhaps for two constructions he made while in exile on Crete. The first is a life-size, hollow wooden cow covered with leather. This he made for Queen Pasiphaë in order to facilitate her seduction of and copulation with a bull that had captured her fancy. The second is the labyrinth, a container for the horrible result of this coupling. An architecture of love and an architecture of death. Both constructions for holding things, containers to be penetrated, bodies.

Giovanni Battista Piranesi, *Le Carceri,* plate 1, first state (ca. 1745)

Giovanni Battista Piranesi, *Le Carceri,* plate 1, second state (ca. 1761)

[MAPPING]

A spherical cell is violated by a line-driven cell. The tail (the line) breaks off. Information flows. The construction begins. The cell-within-a-cell splits and doubles: one into two into four into eight. Now it is a round, bumpy cluster of cells with a void inside. Blastopore [ROCKET]! The outer wall collapses inward at a tiny point. Over the lip of this imploding hole slide streaky layers of differentiated cells—endoderm, mesoderm, notochord. The outside becomes the inside. Gastrulation: invagination, involution, epiboly. How we achieve our tube-within-a-tubeness.

We *are* tubes within tubes (continuous outer-inner surfaces) with intricately articulated interstices. Systems of cells are woven into a dense textile, filling the spaces between inside and outside surface: hierarchies from bone-muscle-nerve-blood vessel to C HOPKINS CaFe, Mighty good, Naturally Clean to quarks and leptons. A section will reveal that the body, the container, is an architecture in the interval.

And like the architecture, the city in "The Lestrygonians" episode, the body is both a static and a changing thing. Listen to Joyce's city: "Trams passing one another, ingoing, outgoing, clanging. . . . Trams in, out. . . . Dignam carted off. Mina Purefoy swollen belly on a bed groaning to have a child tugged out of her. . . . Cityful passing away, other cityful coming, passing away, too: other coming on, passing on. Houses, lines of houses, streets, miles of pavement, piledup bricks, stones (*Ulysses,* 164). Instruments of *passage*, like bodies swallowing food—tubes within tubes.

The artificial cow swallows the woman and the woman swallows the bull. The genetic crisscross bullman is contained by the woman [VESSEL] for a while—a project, in the dark and not seeing, tap-tap-tapping with seeing hands and feet, measuring the world [HYSTERICAL DOCUMENTS]. Later, the labyrinth swallows the bullman and the bullman swallows youths and maidens. As the Lestrygonians swallowed Odysseus' men and as man and beast swallow uncounted bits and bites in this section.

Line

Joyce's text, as all texts are, is composed of lines. Not only lines of text and lines of reference but references to lines, liney words and phrases: *stripling, slender cane, street, wall, line of cane, herringbone tweed, beeline, plait, lines, curves, hair, fibres.* Moreover, it is a text of lines that cross, of intersection—"Do you want to cross?"—and of crossings: the streets crossing, the crossing of the street, the crisscrossing of narration and interior monologue, the crossing of senses (touch and sight). It refers to metaphorical crossing as well: metempsychosis.

The architectonic text is also a complex of lines. The architect uses all manner of lines: lines drawn on paper, lines drawn on earth, plumb lines, imaginary lines between cardinal points, geometry, cables, lines of force. And each of these lines intersects in some way a complex of lines traversing the shortest distance between center and surface of the planet.

Intersecting lines produce points. Intersecting planes produce lines. Intersecting solids produce planes. The intersection is an apparatus for crossing from $n + 1$ dimension to n dimension.

The intersection—the relations among having-been-cuts, sections—is the emblem and tool of the architect. It forms a generic model of architecture, the practice that convention names as being located at the intersection of something called art and something else called science. Making the architectural object requires a manipulation of crossings: the intersection of the force-responsive capabilities of its materials and the forces that act on them, the intersection of functional exigency and formal aesthetic, the intersection of object-maker and object-owner, and other difficult intersections of this kind.

But let us look at the intersection of the making with the representation of the architectural object. Conventionally, when an architect designs an object, he draws it. The architectural object is constructed after the drawings have been made, a crossing from two dimensions to three. Aldo Rossi calls the point of this crossing, the place at which the drawing always stops, "a void which cannot be represented" (*Scientific Autobiography,* 24).

The architect takes in hand a line-shaped, line-making tool and scratches lines on planes. In a reverse dissectional procedure, she makes assemblages of these marks. These are called sections (the set Sections includes the subsets Plans and Elevations); they are the imaginary preliminary residual of cutting an object with a slicing plane—the intersection of a three-dimensional and a two-dimensional object. The result of this intersection is a two-dimensional object, a lacy slice of intersecting ink lines captured by the paper.

The section marks a connection between worlds.

This connection or passage can be modelled by imagining two lines intersecting so that very acute and very obtuse angles are produced. You may recognize here the model of Kasimir Malevich depicting the connection between the material and spiritual worlds. Here, the perspectival vanishing point (the point of intersection) is a door in which the artist may stand and see the world beyond, that world of four dimensions to which the three-dimensional world bears a shadowlike or orthogonal drawing–like resemblance. To traverse the passage between worlds is to come to an end that is as well a beginning. A crossing. A met him pike-hoses.

It is a void which cannot be represented—the place where emptiness and intricacy are the same, the place of perplexing ("thoroughly woven") emptiness. The section (which is an intersection) delineates the here and makes an intersection of theres. It is neither this nor that and it is both this and that.

Point

I do not know the name of the person whom the Charon Leopold Bloom guides across the intersection, the connection between one world and another. It may be collective, blind Homer. It may be poor, crooked-footed Oedipus in herringbone tweed; Oedipus, who could not walk in a beeline, who in fact walked in two lines and jabbed out his own eyes when the lines intersected. But one thing I do assert. That person is an architect, that blind linelike man with black spots in front of his eyes and liney tool in his "seeing hand."

"Queer idea of Dublin he must have, tapping his way round by the stones. Could he walk in a beeline if he hadn't that cane?" At this point, Bloom recalls the name of a weak-eyed, squinting person, a name he had been struggling to recall some twenty-five pages before: "Penrose!"

Over the rational, bipolar logic of the intersection, the blind architect—blind and therefore invisible in the Daedalian world—makes marks on the city with his bobbling, rising and falling tool. Tap, tap, tapping, each tap the instant of intersection of line and plane—a point, a spot. Black spots. [POCHE], black spots on the eye.

Tschumi has located the definition of architecture at the "intersection of logic and pain, rationality and anguish, concept and pleasure"

(*Manhattan Transcripts*, 9). A map of this intersection looks very much like a map of the intersection of those Dublin streets constellated by cane taps. Also like Joyce's triple-tapped poché marked over a text of multiple intersecting lines. T. T. T. Little signs of trabeation: beams on posts. Intersections. Joints.

Bloom's "parallax," in correspondence with Molly's "met him pikehoses" a motif of the chapter, is a two-point view, the sight lines of which intersect in the object, at a point of sectioning. In this fragment of architexture, Joyce has anticipated the Advice (let us spell this word with capital "A") of Louis Zukofsky:

> Light wave and quantum, we have good proof both exist:
> Our present effort is to see how this is: to
> Perfect the composition of a two-point view
>
> . . . .
> Build it. (8:55–56)

Since my response to that section of *Ulysses* was written, I have discovered the identity of the person in the hatch-marked suit, the hatchmark maker, that scrawling scriber who lived in darkness [HATCHERY]. And I was correct: he is an architect. He is also the joint, the connection, who will guide us in the crossing from Joyce's two-dimensional book of the light to Joyce's three-dimensional "book of the dark,"[28] the dream book of Tim Finnegan, the deliriously drunken brick layer on a ladder. Or was it a [LETTER]?

"Who was that masked man?"[29] The Soviet filmmaker Sergei Eisenstein, master of montage, friend of James Joyce, and one of two whom Joyce deemed capable of transferring his work to film, kept in the corner room of his apartment, in the place of an icon, an etching by Giambattista Piranesi, the *Carcere oscura,* or *Dark Prison.*[30]

In an essay about his notion of ecstatic effect in cinema (that makes a significant turn to the etymology of the word: *ex stasis,* "fluidity, flow"), Eisenstein reveals an extraordinary reliance upon Piranesi's visions. In establishing the affiliation between the dissemination upon an emplotment that makes up filmic montage and states of ecstasy/dizziness/exaltation/frenzy, Eisenstein writes:

> De Quincey [Thomas] actually uses Piranesi's own *Prisons* as

Giovanni Battista Piranesi, *Carcere oscura con Antenna pel Suplizio
dé Malfatori* (1743)

the most precise correspondence to those architectural visions which capture him in states of exaltation under the influence of opium: "Many years ago, when I was looking over Piranesi's *Antiquities of Rome,* Mr. Coleridge, who was standing by, described to me a set of plates by that artist, called his *Dreams,* and which record the scenery of his own visions *during* the delirium of a fever: Some of them (I describe only memory of Mr. Coleridge's account) representing vast Gothic halls: on the floor of which stood all sorts of engines and machinery, wheels, cables, pulleys, levers, catapults, *etc., etc.,* expressive of enormous power put forth, and resistance overcome. Creeping along the sides of the walls, you perceived a staircase; and upon it groping his way upwards, was Piranesi himself: follow the stairs a little further, and you perceive it come to a sudden abrupt termination, without any balustrade, and allowing no step onwards to him who had reached the extremity, except into the depths below. Whatever is to become of poor Piranesi, you suppose, at least, that his labours must in some way terminate here. But raise your eyes, and behold a second flight of stairs still higher: on which again Piranesi is perceived, but this time standing on the very brink of the abyss. Again elevate your eye, and a still more aerial flight of stairs is beheld: and again is poor Piranesi busy on his aspiring labours: and so on, until the unfinished stairs and Piranesi both are lost in the upper gloom of the hall. With the same power of endless growth and self-reproduction did my architecture proceed in dreams." . . . We must not be disturbed by factual impreciseness of petty details. The *Prisons* are called *Dreams.* ("Piranesi, or the Fluidity of Forms," 100–101)

In *Philosophy through the Looking Glass,* the French philosopher Jean-Jacques Lecercle explores a vague concept called *délire,* which designates an area of language in which "words are incoherent and meaning fails us" [BABEL]. It is the language of Lewis Carroll, of Raymond Roussel, of *Finnegans Wake.* Lecercle writes:

> *Délire,* then, is at the frontier between two languages, the embodiment of the contradiction between them. Abstract language is systematic; it transcends the individual speaker, separated from

any physical or material origin, it is an instrument of control, mastered by a regulating subject. Material language, on the other hand, is unsystematic, a series of noises, private to individual speakers, not meant to promote communication, and therefore self-contradictory, "impossible" like all "private languages." . . . Language which has reverted to its origin in the human body, where the primary order reigns. (44–45)

Délire is the name and the condition of the overlay. It is the "shady side," the dark, scratched and scrawled part of the prison house. *Délire* is related to *delirium* etymologically but is not synonymous. Lecercle explains that *délire* relates only to a particular form of delirium, "the kind of reflexive 'delirium' in which the patient expounds his system, attempts to go beyond the limits of his madness to introduce method into it, in which also he hesitates between science, after which he strives and for which he longs, and the wildest fiction" (1). Marguerite Yourcenar, writing on the *Carceri*, construes Piranesi as drawing along the lines of délire:

Everything in these *Prisons* suggests that Piranesi had attempted in a lucid state to rationalize images which had perhaps lost the manifest meaning they possessed in his delirium, to justify their title by adding to these transcendental dungeons and dizzying torture chambers some unimpeachable detail of real dungeons and actual tortures—in short, to replace on the level of concepts and comprehensible emotions of the waking state, darker but also less unexpected, what had initially been the prodigious hallucination of an architect, the dream of a builder drunk on pure volumes, pure space. (*Dark Brain,* 108)

Lecercle continues: "Mere delirium is poor and repetitive: this other type, . . . *délire,* is rich and imaginative; it calls for the respect and attention of the man of science, the psychologist, and the philosopher" (*Philosophy through the Looking Glass,* 1–2).

The French word for what we call a parapet is *garde-fou.* The function of the parapet, then, if I may be so Viconian, is to guard the mad, to keep the delirious from jumping from the heights into the abyss. Architecture contains madness.

Délire is one joint between the fields of the constructions of Piranesi and Joyce. There are others.

Giovanni Battista Piranesi, *Le Carceri*, plate 6, second state (ca. 1761)

In the second state *Carceri,* Piranesi rationalizes over the etchings of the first state, drawn in his delirious fever. The scratchings and hatch marks are multiplied, rendering these etchings much darker. In the second state etchings, greater emphasis is given to depictions of instruments: horrible machines suggesting the apparatuses of torture. These gruesome devices are absent in the original etchings. But look closely. These are tools of construction: pulleys, winches, ladders, carpenters' trestles, jacks, and scaffolding. The Prisons are *Work in Progress.*[31]

Before these dark and secret visions, we are in the presence of a dream. Yourcenar insists:

> No connoisseur of oneiric matters will hesitate a moment in the presence of these drawings evincing all the chief characteristics of the dream state: negation of time, incoherence of space, suggested levitation, intoxication of the impossible reconciled or transcended, terror closer to ecstasy than is assumed by those who analyze the visionary's creations from outside, absence of visible contact between the dream's parts or characters, and finally a fatal and necessary beauty. (*Dark Brain,* 110)

Piranesi's entire oeuvre mimes the construction of *Finnegans Wake.* As Yourcenar has pointed out, "The subjects of Piranesi's descriptive engravings fall into two categories, which of course intersect" (*Dark Brain,* 96). The two categories are the baroque edifices(overlapping geometries) and the bits and pieces of centuries-old ruins (the debris of history and culture). Emplotment and dissemination.

The *Pianta di ampio magnifico Collegio,* the sole building plan invention that has come to us from Piranesi, is emblematic. Circle inscribed in square, Viconian four-fold circle, "great square wheel," overlapping geometries with intricate interstitial spaces, it is a *carcere,* a *mise en abîme.* The essential and the polysemous superimposed. A dissemination upon an emplotment.

In the *Collegio,* type is subjected to irony. A topological space may be projected from a reading of a drawing that (almost) adheres to type. In and out, moving along the surfaces. Playing a game. I sense the vague presence of a wandering goose.

The *abîme* of de Quincey's recollection of the *Prisons* is, in manifold multiplication, a major structuring element of *Finnegans Wake.* The adult male father figure in the *Wake,* whose initials are HCE and whose name might be Humphrey Chimpden Earwicker, but is also and perhaps more appropriately Here Comes Everybody, appears throughout the text in layers of reflexive situations, much as Piranesi's, or de Quincey's, or, rather, Coleridge's stairs. If we dissect out a layer, we see him appearing and reappearing as the fallen one: Adam, Napoleon, Icarus, Tim Finnegan, Lucifer (the light bearer who fell to darkness), even Humpty Dumpty. Fictional and historical events slide into thematic identity to such a degree that it is impossible to separate them. (We might make a comparison here to Piranesi's *Campo Marzio.*) So do substances and objects: tea, urine, post and beam, Christ crucified. Words slide into each other as well. (Joyce owned a painting of the city of Cork in a cork frame.) Things become identical based on properties of their structure. You may recognize here the Freudian mechanisms of condensation and displacement in the dream. You may also recognize a part of the program of topology.

   Finnegans Wake is abîme within abîme, abîme intersecting abîme. Here is an example: In the "joint" offered at the beginning falls one of many homophonic iterations of a quotation from the French historian Edgar Quinet, a proponent of Vico's theory of history. The original quotation is lifted from Quinet's *Introduction à la philosophie de l'humanité* and appears nearly intact on page 281 of the *Wake* (in the notoriously obscure section that dances on the interface between Euclidean and non-Euclidean geometry and alludes to the compass many times). Recall the joint: "type by tope, letter from litter, word at ward, with sendence of sundance, since the days of Plooney and Columcellas when Giacinta, Pervenche and Margaret swayed over the all-too-ghoulish and illyrical and innumantic in our mutter nation" (*FW,* 615.1–4). Here is Quinet. Hear the identity: *"Aujourd'hui comme aux temps de Pline et de Columelle la jacinthe se plaît dans les Gaules, la pervenche en Illyrie, la marguerite sur les ruines de Numance et pendant qu'autour d'elles les villes ont changé de maîtres et de noms"* (*FW,* 281.4–8).

   More than the homophony matters here, however. The complete Quinet passage points out that underneath the collisions of civilizations and the broken residual detritus of the history of humankind lies the continuous cycle of wildflowers: history as a dissemination upon an emplotment. Quinet's quotation appears, deformed and adulterated, numerous times throughout *Finnegans Wake.* The name of Quinet appears only once, on page 117, just before a description of the fate of the aforementioned letter (it was eaten and disseminated in excrement upon the ground where it was scratched up and recovered—recycled—by a [HEN] who may or may not have been the author of the [LETTER]).

And look in what company lies the name of Quinet: "From quiqui quinet to michemiche chelet and a jambebatiste to a brulobrulo!" (*FW*, 117.11–12). Edgar Quinet, Jules Michelet, Giambattista Vico, and Giordano Bruno: theorists of the circle. The four points of the square in which is described the circle of *Finnegans Wake*. Bruno presented his magical circular memory system in a book called *Shadows*. Michelet translated Vico's *Scienza Nuova* into French, and his introduction contains the ideas used in *Finnegans Wake*.

Michelet also provides a connection to the contemporary philosopher Michel Serres, whose interdisciplinary weavings are constructed upon the loom of the thermodynamic model. In Serres' *Hermes* appear two adjacent essays, "Michelet: The Soup" and "Language and Space: From Oedipus to Zola." The two are connected by the closing paragraph of the first, in which Serres writes, "The strategy of criticism is located in the object of criticism" (38). This is tantamount to Derrida's "There is nothing outside the text." (Find your instrument in the text.)

In "Language and Space," Serres suggests that the structuring apparatus of Zola's entire *Rougon Macquart* series is the *jeu de l'oie*, the [GAME] of goose [UNDESIRABLE BEASTS]. In addition to being connected by name to certain architectural types, the motifs of the game constitute, as Serres points out, the elementary program of topology: closed, open, connective path, tear, continuous, discontinuous, threshold, limit. The jeu de l'oie is the interface of typology and topology. So is the body. Serres: "My body (I cannot help it) is not plunged into a single, specified space. It works in Euclidean space, but it only works there. It sees in a projective space; it touches, caresses, and feels in a topological space" (44).

It is easy to find the goose's game—a dissemination upon an emplotment—in Joyce's text. Clues abound, perhaps most significantly for present purposes in the phrase "as game as your goose" (123.29), which appears in the same sentence as a reference to the "Rime of the Ancient Mariner," the work of Samuel Taylor Coleridge and a tale of the sea, *la mer*.

"The sea is mother: *la Mer, c'est la mère*," writes Serres in "Miche-

Giovanni Battista Piranesi, *Le Carceri*, plate 3, second state (ca. 1761)

Giovanni Battista Piranesi, *Le Carceri,* plate 4, second state (ca. 1761)

let: The Soup." Between them, Serres and Michelet describe the sea as a prebiotic soup constantly being heated by two rings (circles) of active volcanoes—one in the Atlantic, one in the Pacific—and therefore constantly being stirred in circles upon the sphere by a resulting giant Carnot cycle and by the spirals of storms and cyclones. Circles of circles. Serres via Michelet then goes on to see this world through geometry, mechanics, physics, chemistry, and biology, where it becomes a static machine, a compression engine, an electrical engine, a chemical machine with "points of condensation and cycles of displacement" (34), and finally an organism, which, with its rounded geometry, double rings producing nourishing milk-soup and blood-soup flowing in cycles tracing those of the moon, is female. La mer, c'est la mère. A perfectly Joycean plot. "And to find a locus for an alp get a howlth on her bayrings as a prisme O and for a second O unbox your compasses" (FW, 287.8–11).

Which brings us back around to the point, or joint, of beginning. The compass is a sewing instrument as well. It is the instrument of Joyce's "sewing circle," his great "engine with one square wheel," "our wholemole millwheeling vicociclometer," the disseminative circle that is the text of the world. In the second state of plate 4 of the Carceri, Piranesi etched over the top of the great free-standing column a St. Catherine's Wheel, a whirling circle for flinging flashes of light into the darkness.

> For that (the rapt one warns) is what papyr is meed of, made of, hides and hints and misses in prints. Til ye finally (though not yet endlike) meet with the acquaintance of Mister Typus, Mistress Tope and all the little typtopies. Fillstup. So you need hardly spell me how every word will be bound over to carry three score and ten toptypsical readings throughout the book of Doublends Jined (may his forehead be darkened with mud who would sunder!) til Daleth, mahomahouma, who oped it closeth thereof the. Dor. (20.10–18)[32]

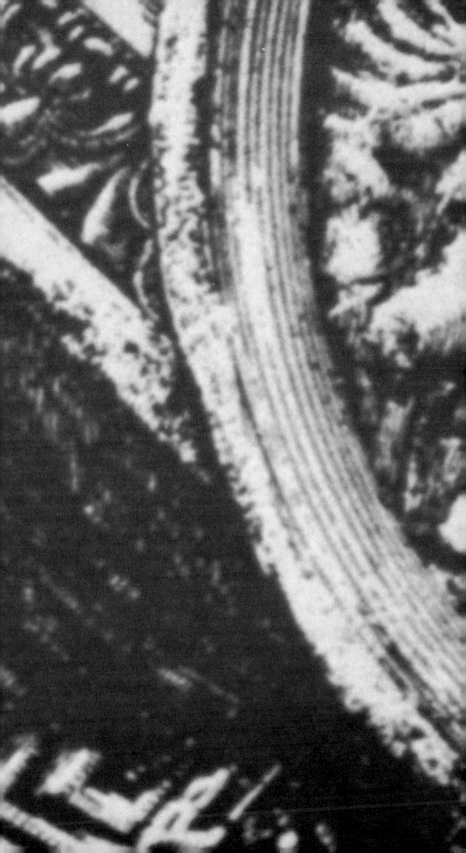

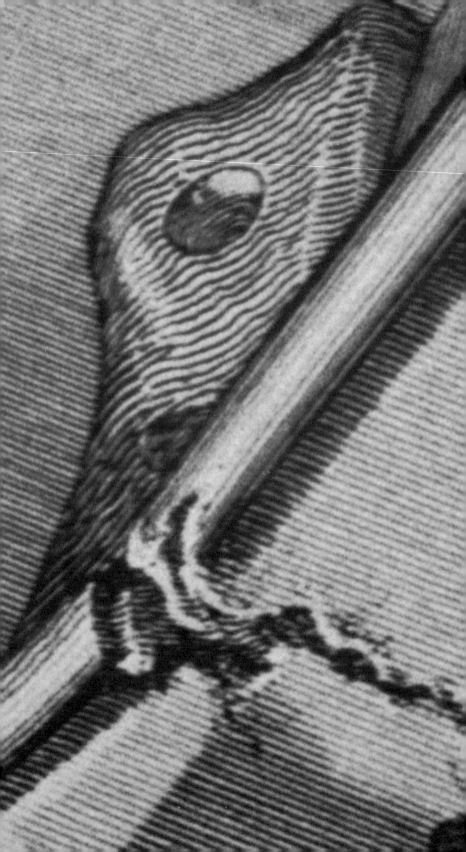

Chapter 3

Construction Three-Plus-One: The House That Jack Built

(Un Chateau des Cartes)

THIS IS the [HOUSE] and museum of SIR JOHN SOANE, R.A., architect. Soane was born in 1753, the son of a small country builder, and died, after a long and distinguished career, in 1837. He lived here for the last twenty-four years of his life (1813–1837). Previously, he had lived next door in No. 12, which he had designed for himself in 1792. This and the corresponding house on the east (No. 14) are both Soane's work, and the three houses together make a balanced composition towards the fields.
(*A Short Description of Sir John Soane's Museum*)

"THIS the way to the museyroom. Mind your hats goan in!" Through the looking glass: emerge from the dark concavity out onto the convex surface. Where you are is where you are going. Bull's-eye! "Now yiz are in the Willingdone Museyroom" (*FW*, 8.10).

At five o'clock in the morning on 18 March 1778, the twenty-four-year-old student John Soane set out from London to Italy. Some months later, braving his poor Italian, he presented himself at the studio of Giambattista Piranesi in Rome. Piranesi, eaten up with an unspeakable disease and weeks away from the end of four decades of frenzied line drawing, was apparently impressed. Soane carried away with him four etchings from Piranesi's *Vedute di Roma*.

"THIS IS the Hausman all paven and stoned, that cribbed the Cabin that never was owned that cocked his leg and hennad his Egg" [UNDESIRABLE BEASTS] (*FW*, 205.34–36).

THIS IS the Picture Room. This is a hidden compartment. This wall swings out. Behind it is another that swings out. On the other side of this swinging wall, there is a recess, the floor of which drops to the Monk's Parlour (the "Parloir of Padre Giovanni") in the basement. At the back of the recess is a large window receiving light from the interior court that is the Monk's Yard. Framed and framing the opening between the Picture Room and the recess that frames the spectacle of the window beyond, are the four etchings that Piranesi, "one of the two greatest architectural draughtsmen of the eighteenth century," the guidebook to his house assures us, gave to the young Soane. In addition, nestled within and upon the walls of the recess are two enormous etchings from the *Vedute* and fifteen ink and wash drawings, originals for the etchings that Francesco Piranesi published shortly after his father's death.[1]

John Soane kept Piranesi in the closet. If we slice through numbers 12 and 13 *Lincoln's Inn Fields* (a LIFfey kind of place), we can see a resemblance to "Thirty-two West Eleventh streak" that goes far beyond the numerical resemblance of address (12/13 and 32/11, which, in addition to the acronymic point of resemblance, the architect of the latter would have found highly significant).[2] The Piranesi scratchings are contained within the [POCHE] of the house that Soane built. The section becomes a text that can then be read, that is, misread or rewritten. The information provided by the section is always incomplete.

> And look at this prepronominal *funferal*, engraved and retouched and edgewiped and pudden-padded, very like a whale's egg farced with pemmican, as were it sentenced to be nuzzled over a full trillion times for ever and a night till his noddle sink or swim by that ideal reader suffering from an ideal insomnia: all those red raddled obeli cayennepeppercast over the text, calling unnecessary attention to errors, omissions, repetitions, and misalignments. (*FW*, 120.9–16)

If we dissect out the pattern of letter T's from *Finnegans Wake*, we have one of the important generative sections of the work. Triple tapped poché. T. T. T. Beams on posts. Trabeation. Patterns of black marks in front of the eye. Apparatus. "One cannot help noticing that rather more than half of the lines run north-south in the Nemzes and Bukarahast directions while the others go west-east in search from Maliziies with Bulgrad for, tiny tot though it looks when schtschupnistling alongside other incunabula, it has its cardinal points for all that" (*FW*, 114.2–7).

The poché at no. 13 is not uniform on the vertical. There are strange disjunctions, holes in this architecture: slivers of space, shafts of light. There is here an intangible but sensible construction that exists within the material construction. "Soane designed this house to live in, but also as a setting for his antiquities and works of art" (*Short Description*, 1).

"IN reality the whole of creation is language, and so is literally created by the word, the created and creating word itself. . . . But the letter is inextricably bound up with this word both in general and in particular. . . . All the plastic arts: architecture, sculpture, painting, etc., belong pre-eminently among such script, and developments and derivations of it." Walter Benjamin portrayed allegory as being fragmentary, ambiguous, palimpsestic, and [HIEROGLYPH]ic. For him, allegory involves misreading and is therefore potentially critical; it fosters a disregard for aesthetic boundaries, especially between visual and verbal categories; it is made by the "piling up of fragments ceaselessly"; and it emerges from "an appreciation of the transience of things, and the concern to rescue them for eternity" (*Origin*, 187).

Fredric Jameson distinguishes Benjamin's concept of allegory from the traditional one:

> The allegorical spirit is profoundly discontinuous, a matter of
> breaks and heterogeneities, of the multiple polysemia of the dream
> rather than the homogeneous representation of the symbol. Our
> traditional concept of allegory . . . [is] a one-dimensional view
> of this signifying process, which might only be set in motion
> and complexified were we willing to entertain the more alarming
> notion that such equivalences are themselves in constant change
> and transformation at each perpetual present of the text. ("Third-
> World Literature," 71)

THIS IS the Dressing Room, a small room that connects the Study to the Corridor. Surmounting the dispersion of antique marbles, Renaissance bronzes, and small pictures, above either of the two facing doorways are busts of Andrea Palladio and Inigo Jones, Soane's formidable fathers, looking down upon him, far below and naked. The anxiety of influence concretized and embedded in the construction. "Allegorical personification has always concealed the fact that its function is not the personification of things, but rather to give the concrete a more imposing form by getting it up as a person" (*Origin*, 187).

THIS IS the Monument Yard, a tiny court at the heart of the Museum.

"Mememormee!" (*FW*, 628.14).

IN its fully developed, baroque form allegory brings with it its own court; the profusion of emblems is grouped around the figural center, which is never absent from genuine allegories, as opposed to periphrases of concepts. They seem to be arranged in an arbitrary way: *The confused "court"*—the title of a Spanish *Trauerspiel*—could be adopted as the model of allegory. This court is subject to the law of "dispersal" and "collectedness." (*Origin*, 188)

THIS IS the Breakfast Room. John Soane wrote: "The views from this room into the Monument Court and into the Museum, the mirrors in the ceiling, and the looking-glasses, combined with the variety of outline and general arrangement and the design and decoration of this limited space, present a succession of those fanciful effects which constitute the poetry of architecture" (quoted in Summerson et al., *John Soane*, 34). IN this house, Soane anticipates Roman Jakobson: the poetic becomes the projection of the metaphoric axis onto the metonymic, the intersection of synchrony and diachrony. It is the superimposition of a dissemination and an emplotment. "The [LETTER]! The litter!" "Problem ye ferst, construct ann aquilittoral dryankle Probe loom! With his primal handstoe in his sole salivarium. Concoct an equoangular trilitter. [As Rhombulus and Rhebus went building rhomes one day]" (*FW*, 286.19–22 and n.1).

IN THE Breakfast Room, on the south wall, is a shrine to Napoleon. Here are two portraits of Napoleon, one executed in the same year that Soane's and Piranesi's paths crossed, and the other at the other end of Napoleon's life, when he was exiled on the Isle of Elba. Between the two portraits is a photograph of a pistol with the words *L'Empereur Napoleon* engraved on its barrel. The pistol itself, which was stolen from the museum in 1969, may only be associated with Napoleon through its script, for the engraved words are a pawnbroker's ruse.[3]

THIS IS a Prooshious gunn. This is a ffrinch. Tip. This is the flag the Prooshious, the Cap and Soracer. This is the bullet that byng the flag of the Prooshious. This is the ffrinch that fire on the Bull that bang the flag of the Prooshious. Saloos the Crossgunn! Up with your pike and fork! Tip. (Bullsfoot! Fine!) This is the triplewon hat of Lipoleum. Tip. Lipoleumhat. (*FW*, 8.10–16)

THIS IS the Dome, the central area of the Museum. "This, already completed while Soane was living at No. 12 and therefore the oldest part of the present Museum, is a kind of Grotto of Antiquities, perhaps inspired by the romantic engravings of G. B. Piranesi" (*Short Description*, 6). "From this brilliantly lit room, Light filters down to the ground floor, and, on the north, still further down to the otherwise completely obscure [CRYPT]" (Summerson et al., *John Soane*, 36).

THIS IS the Crypt. It is a dark place, the underground chamber, the vesicle, the secret place, the place of secretions. "All he could see was a labyrinth of lines crossing and recrossing each other, which covered the paper so thickly that it was difficult to discern the blank spaces between them. 'Read it,' said the officer. 'I can't,' said the explorer. 'Yet it's clear enough,' said the officer'" (Kafka, *Penal Colony*, 202).

THIS IS the Sepulchral Chamber, the lowest level of the Dome's great shaft. IN THE center of the Chamber is the sarcophagus of Seti I. The monolithic vessel is covered within and without with incised [HIERO-GLYPH]ics. Hidden inside, on the bottom, are incised chapters seventy-two and eighty-nine from the *Book of the Dead*.

"There's something behind the *Bug of the Deaf*" (*FW*, 134.36).[4]

IN THE basement of the Soane house, reached by traversing the Sepulchral Chamber from the Crypt, moving from beneath no. 13 to beneath no. 12, are the Catacombs, so-called because, in the beginning, the room was lined with niches containing cinerary urns. Now there are three cinerary urns placed against the south wall. One of them once belonged to Giambattista Piranesi.

Circling back by the Sepulchral Chamber and passing between the Crypt and the Monument Court floor, we arrive at the bottom of the basement stairs and find ourselves . . .

IN THE "Parloir de Padre Giovanni." On the south side of the Parlor, the ceiling disappears and the space of the room slides up between the recess containing the work of Giovanni Battista and the unfolding, booklike walls above. Beyond this niche of sliding space, through the window before us, is an outdoor room of bizarre assemblage, including a monumental construction made of a great miscellany of building fragments.

THIS IS the Monk's Yard and the Monk's Tomb. Of this place, Soane wrote: "The tomb of the monk adds to the gloomy scenery of this hallowed place, wherein attention has been given to very minute circumstance. The pavement, composed of the tops and bottoms of broken bottles, and pebbles found amongst the gravel dug out for the foundations of the monastery, and disposed in symmetry of design, furnishes an admirable lesson of simplicity and economy, and shows the unremitting assiduity of the pious monk" (quoted in Summerson, *New Description*, 29–30).

IN THE year in which Soane began work on no. 13, Johann Wilhelm Ritter wrote, "IN THE context of allegory the image is only a signature, only the monogram of essence, not the essence itself in a mask. But there is nothing subordinate about written script; it is not cast away in reading, like dross. It is absorbed along with what is read, as its 'pattern' " (quoted in Benjamin, *Origin*, 214–215).

Soane again, that is, John Soane, son of John Soan, a bricklayer: "It may, perhaps, be asked, before leaving this part of the Museum, at what period the Monk existed whose memory is here preserved, and whether he is to be identified with any of those whose deeds have enshrined their names. The answer to these questions is furnished by Horace: *Dulce est desipere in loco*" (quoted in Summerson, *New Description*, 30).

It is delightful to be nonsensical in a fitting place.

(THIS IS the house that Padre Giovanni built.)

THIS IS the priest all shaven and shorn, that roundheaded Neapolitan with the circular signature: Jack Vico, who could no more reconcile his circle with the square of Descartes than could his devotee, Jack Piranesi, two decades later, or the academicians two centuries later. The problem of squaring the circle would be left to Jack Joyce. IN THE house that Jack built, the squares are not squares and the circles are not circles.[5] "For I've flicked up all the crambs as they crumbed from your table um, singing glory allaloserem, cog it out, here goes a sum. So read we in must book. It tells. He prophets most who bilks the best" (*FW*, 304.35–305.2).

"IN order for a part of the past to be touched by the present, there must be no continuity between them" (Benjamin, "N," *Passagen-Werk*, N7:7).

"Is the strays world moving mound or what static [BABEL] is this, tell us?" (*FW*, 499.33–34).

IN THE wide space of architecture, that which is not the building is of no consequence. Ideas, descriptions, critiques, theories, even ideology—all abstractions—are, in the end, passive and inert, the ether of the architectural space. The object—separate and privileged—is the sole subject of an enclosed and centripetal order. Architecture is a collection of ruins that closes at six o'clock. (Segrest and Bloomer, "Without Architecture," i).

The museum is the place of preservation of the dead, the authoritative, the valued. It is the place of the power of the Father. (John Soane, the Master Builder, bitterly disappointed with the way his two sons conducted their lives, de-soaned them by leaving his house as a museum of architecture.) The muses are invisible, hiding away in the [POCHE]. The museum is quiet, static, clean.

But *this* museum is full of junk, full of debris, fragmented and untidy, "like a children's nursery" (Benjamin, *Origin*, 188). Remember The House O'Shea:

The warped flooring of the lair and soundconducting walls thereof, to say nothing of the uprights and imposts, were persianly literatured with burst loveletters, telltale stories, stickyback snaps, doubtful eggshells, bouchers, flints, borers, puffers, amygdaloid almonds, rindless raisins, alphybettyformed verbage, vivlical viasses, ompiter dictas, visus umbique, ahems and ahahs, imeffible tries at speech unasyllabled, you owe mes, eyoldhyms, fluefoul smut, fallen lucifers, vestas which had served, showered ornaments, borrowed brogues, reversibles jackets, blackeye lenses, family jars, falsehair shirts, Godforsaken scapulars, neverworn breeches, cutthroat ties, counterfeit franks, best intentions, curried notes, upset latten tintacks, unused mill and stumpling stones, twisted quills, painful digests, magnifying wineglasses, solid objects cast at goblins, once current puns, quashed quotatoes, messes of mottage, unquestionable issue papers, seedy ejaculations. (*FW*, 183.8–23)

"IN THE ruin history has physically merged into the setting. And in this guise history does not assume the form of the process of an eternal life so much as that of irresistible decay" (Benjamin, *Origin,* 177).

IN THE Picture Room, high up, you may have noticed a painting by Sir Francis Bourgeois, entitled *A* [HEN] *Defending Her Chickens.* "THIS IS the jinnies with their legahorns feinting to read in their handmade's book of stralegy while making their war undisides the Willingdone" (*FW,* 8.31–33). THIS IS "the hen that crowed on the turrace of [BABEL]" (199.30).

(After six o'clock) the chickens enter the [HOUSE] to eat the malt. They peck, they hatch, they cackle, they scratch, they mess things up. They produce objectionable odors [UNDESIRABLE BEASTS].

THIS IS the [HATCHERY]. It is a place of production, flow, desire, signifiers on the cheep. It is chaotic, dynamic, dirty. There is no author-ity. It is the place of hatching—hatching lines of [POCHE]—and the place of hatches—small doors opening into dark places. The gesture of hatching a drawing is also a kitchen gesture: the French verb *hacher* denotes both these things, as well as the act of hacking something to bits. The hatchery bears the trace of architectural terrorism, "as sure as herself pits hen to paper and there's scribings scrawled on eggs" (*FW,* 615.9–10). Here, in this smooth space, plots are hatched.

"Rockaby, [BABEL], flatten a wall" (278.L4).

"A feminist architecture is not architecture at all" (unauthorized quotation).[6]

THIS IS the House That Jill (*ou Gilles, peut-être?*) Built. ("Which title is the true-to-type motto-in-lieu for that Tick for Teac thatchment painted witt wheth one darkness?"; *FW,* 139.29–30).

"Tip (Bullseye! Game!) How Copenhagen ended. This way the museyroom. Mind your boots goan out" (10.21–23).

Postscrypt
And here are the details
Finnegans Wake, 611.3

The drawing presented here is a superimposition of a diagram that appears on page 293 of *Finnegans Wake* on the façade of nos. 12–13–14 Lincoln's Inn Fields. Joyce's diagram is the vesica piscis, the Euclidean apparatus for the generation of an equilateral triangle. This apparatus is effected

Superimposition of the *Vesica Piscis* upon the (ideal) façade of Sir John Soane's House and Museum by means of the compasses, the instrument and invention of the architect and the instrument of authority. The diagram itself is emblematic of rational man; but inscribed within, superimposed over and bounding the central no. 13, is the feminine triangle, designated *alpha-lambda-pi,* or "ALP," the initials of Anna Livia Plurabelle, the feminine figure of the *Wake.*

This constructed text sets up the duality of the museum (the place where objects assigned value by authority are preserved and a hallowed architectural type) and the [HATCHERY] (a kind of construction, but not an architectural type, a concept that is figured by generative processes) and poses Soane's [HOUSE] (a collection of architectural debris not dissimilar to Piranesi's oeuvre) as the interface. The [CRYPT] is the critical joint. It belongs to the museum, but is a monad of the hatchery: a mined field, a holey space, a [VESSEL]. The inscriptions (the encrypted) of the hatchery undermine the foundations of the museum [THE PROPER].

In *Finnegans Wake,* the joint between the museum as the locus of preservation and exhibition and as a place of flow occurs in Joyce's invocation of the Battle of Waterloo. Here, in the most Freudian manner, the museum of the "Lipoleum" and the "Willingdone" slips into the place of micturition and excrement. For *this* textual construction, the joint between Joyce's museum and Soane's is the vesica piscis, the fish's bladder, with all puns intended.

Another joint is the bull's eye. The museum is entered through the prominent and disorienting bull's-eye mirror on Soane's stair and exited (through Joyce's text) with the exclamation "Bullseye! Game!" that closes the "Museyroom" section of the *Wake.* The connections of the bull's eye, the [MIRROR], and the strange [POCHE] of Joyce's [LETTER] constitute one of the structural systems of this text. We might call this a section—a concept that swerves from the Vitruvian concept of *scenographia* (which depends on the eye as instrument of the gaze, rather than as encrypted flow). This section can be approximated by two appropriations. One is from Jurij Lotman: "a construction of a pattern of intersections" (intersections defined as ruptures in a system that mark its collision with another system; *Semiotics,* 71). The other, intersecting neatly with the first, is from Marcel Duchamp: *"un Repos capable de pires excentricités"* (a rest capable of the worst eccentricities; quoted in *Duchamp's Notes,* 152).

Other examples of such sections are the constellations "THIS IS" and "IN THE." "THIS IS" is a metonymical figure of the nursery rhyme "The House That Jack Built" (which, as Guy Davenport tells us, connects Joyce and John Ruskin through the labyrinth; see *Geography of the Imagination*). Mirroring Joyce's "museyroom" section, it serves, at the same time, as a form of structural poché for the textual construction here. "IN THE" signifies enterability by the reader. It also refers to the grand allegorical construction of Walter Benjamin, the *Passagen-Werk*. (The "IN" is also the "N" that provides the poché of Benjamin's construction, and some "IN" appropriations that appear here are lifted from the "N" of the *Passagen-Werk*.)

Architecture's resistance to narrativity suggests the possibility of a connection to allegory, which indicates both form and technique, hovering between sign and symbol and between the embrace of history and its denial, a counternarrative (but not antinarrative) device. Because of its relation to temporality, narrative itself is uniquely literary. Yet, as Paul Ricoeur points out, its trace remains in the concept of emplotment. The plot described by Ricoeur smacks of the architectonic. The plot of which he writes is architecture, though not building. Besides being architectonic constructions, plots, like architecture, are both singular and nonsingular, both submissive to paradigms and deviant from established models, both in conformity with tradition and in rebellion against paradigms from the tradition (see *Time and Narrative*). This concept of emplotment—with its relation to structure— will allow us to counter simplistic (metaphorical) notions of narrative in architecture without disposing of the idea altogether.

In literary texts where the chronological structure of narrative is faded or indistinct, the reader must construct the narrative by sifting through the debris of the text. In these works (good examples are Thomas Pynchon's *V.* and Vladimir Nabokov's *Pale Fire*), meaning resides in relations of parts and structures—or apparatus—of the text rather than in explicit narrative content. At the point where meaning lies not in a one-to-one relation between thing and concept but in a constructive operation upon many possible connections at many levels of scale (letter, word, sentence, paragraph, plot), the literary work not only begins to bear a resemblance to architecture (which is "illegible" in a similar way that such texts are "illegible") but also becomes a model of what architecture might be.

In *Finnegans Wake* the operations that necessarily bound a text— writing and reading—constitute the substance of the text to such a degree that the narrativity of the text (the story, the representation) nearly disappears. The ostensible object—the narrative—is strung out, thin, and incidental to the substantial, monumental object: the two great enclosing parentheses (reading and [re]writing) that constitute the essential narrativity. Reading this text must be a rewriting, or misreading, for Joyce has waived any rights to authority with respect to meaning and representation. Ambiguity not only runs rampant; it is the rule.

Like [THE PROPER] book of Joyce with its satisfactory size, weight, and not unpleasant cover, Piranesi's drawings can sit easily in picture galleries or in entrance halls among our other possessions. They become framed and frozen, owned things of so much finite surface, so much beauty, so much value. But, as I have tried to show, the tiniest beginning of incision into these surfaces initiates multitudinous pathways and possibilities of decoding and recoding.

These works are littered with traces of another Jack: non-bipolar logic, recurring themes, submerged allusion, absence of beginnings or endings, intensification of the difference in the written and the spoken, and the continual play of polysemy and ambiguity. ("And shall not Babel be with Lebab? And he war"; *FW*, 258.11–12.)[7]

In these constructions, reading and writing approach identity. In encoding, Joyce and Piranesi were decoding; in constructing their texts, Piranesi and Joyce were deconstructing the texts of Western culture; in decoding or deconstructing these texts, readers necessarily construct codes themselves. These codes take the forms of apparatus, or machines, which contain within them the ghost of architecture. "In the fields with which we are concerned, knowledge comes only in flashes. The text is the thunder rolling long afterward" (Benjamin, "N," *Passagen-Werk*, N1:1).

Ar

Gratia

Grat

Lacus

Syllapsies

The end of linear writing is indeed the end of the book, even if, even today, it is within the form of a book that new writings— literary or theoretical—allow themselves to be, for better or for worse, encased.

Jacques Derrida, *Of Grammatology*

Graspings (*syllapsies*): wholes and not wholes, convergent divergent, consonant dissonant, from all things one and from one thing all.

Heraclitus, Fragment CXXIV

This appendix serves as a "switching mechanism" for alternate readings of this book. Below, there are twenty-two motifs that are both generative themes and connectives. The motifs appear in the main text in bracketed capital letters; they serve to direct the reader either to this section or to other locations in the text that are encoded by the same word. The syllapsies also serve as supplemental reading aids; these words and their motifs are "hints" (as in "hides and hints and misses in prints") that constitute reading "joints."

BABEL

All the languages are present, for they have not yet been separated. It's a tower of Babel.

James Joyce on *Finnegans Wake*

Finnegans Wake is a *tour de Babel*: a tower of Babble and a tour of language. Also a wheel of chatter (*tour du babil*). Babble is incoherent speech: glossolalia, speaking in tongues, the language of the body. Whether a cry or *écrit,* it is improper. The Tower of Babel is a joint between architecture and language. In the beginning of the *Antichità Romane,* Piranesi gives us a pair of spiraling towers; in plan, each would resemble Brancusi's 1929 drawing *Symbol of Joyce.*

> August 13 1979. . . . I followed all the Babelian indications in *Finnegans Wake* and yesterday I wanted to take the plane to Zurich and read out loud sitting on his knees, starting with the beginning (Babel, the fall, and the Finno-Phoenician motif, *"the fall (bababadalgh)* [1] *[. . .].* [2] *The great fall of the offwall entailed at such short notice the pftjschute of Finnegan [. . .] Phall if you but will, rise you must: and none so soon either shall the pharce for the nunce come to a setdown secular phoenish . . .")* up to the passage on Gigglotte's Hill and the Babbyl Malket toward the end, passing through *"The babbelers with their thangas vain have been (confusium hold them!) [. . .] Who ails tongue coddeau, aspace of dumbillsilly? And they fell upong one another: and themselves they have fallen . . ."* and through *"This battering babel allower the door and sideposts . . ."* and the entire page up to *"Filons, filoosh! Cherchons la flamme! Fammfamm! Fammfamm!"* through that passage that you know better than anyone (p. 164) and in which I all of a sudden discover *"the babbling pumpt of platinism,"* through that other one around the *"turrace of Babbel,"* the entire passage about Anna Livia Plurabelle, translated in part, in which you will find things that are absolutely unheard of; and that everything that comes around *"A and aa ab ad abu abiad. A babbel men dub gulch of tears."* or around *"And shall not Babel be with Lebab? And he war. And he shall open his mouth and answer: I hear, O Ismael . . . and he deed . . ."* up to *"O Loud . . . Loud . . . Ha he hi ho hu. Mummum."* I draw out the text, as one says of actors, at least up to *"Usque! Usque! Usque! Lignum in . . . Is the strays world moving mound or what static babel is this, tell us?"* (Derrida, *Post Card,* 240–241)

The connections among babel, babble, and falling should not go unnoted.

How remarkably Joyce's (Viconian) thunder words resemble the mouthed sounds of my infant ("without speech," a babbler) daughter: "baba-

badalgharagh . . ." The sounds she makes emerge from her mouth but origi-
nate from a variety of depths within her body, conveying the different moods
that her corresponding facial gestures suggest.

> Vico's account of human genesis anticipatorily encompasses
> Freud's, finally, by understanding that human consciousness, lan-
> guage, and reality genetically unfold from inside the bodies of
> infants. Although the decorous civilization of Vico's Europe had
> begun learning to devalue the human body, nothing in the uni-
> verse known to Vico's gentile man ever happens outside of its
> space, within which the human world and its knowing aborigi-
> nally and always come to be. (Bishop, *Book of the Dark*, 193)

CRYPT

A crypt is a gland, a follicle, a body [VESSEL], a hiding place, a
holey space, a place of petrification [STONE], a space of melancholy. It is a
dark, inky place. It is the place of secrets and secretions.

Mark Wigley, reading Derrida reading Nicholas Abraham and
Maria Torok on the psychoanalytic phenomenon of "refusing to mourn,"
approaches succinctly the place of secretions:

> This "act of vomiting to the inside" defines a secret vault within
> the subject, a "crypt" constructed by the libidinal forces of the
> traumatic scene which "through their contradiction, through
> their very opposition support the internal resistance of the vault
> like pillars, beams, studs, and retaining walls, leaning the powers
> of intolerable pain against an ineffable, forbidden pleasure"
> [Derrida]. . . . The crypt organizes the space in which it cannot
> simply be placed, and sustains the topography it fractures. These
> fractures, however, are not new. They have been present in the
> topography ever since the original traumatic scene, organizing
> the self and making possible the illusion that the scene never oc-
> curred. . . . The crypt is constructed because of the impossibility
> of using language in the normal way, by exchanging words for
> a certain object in voicing grief, without revealing a shameful
> secret: "the impossibility of expressing, of placing words onto
> the market" [Derrida]. Nevertheless, it hides itself within the
> marketplace as another kind of contract, organizing an-other

operation of language. *Even while keeping its secret, the crypt leaks.* ("Postmortem Architecture, 168–170; emphasis mine)

One of the undesirable Piranesis that occupy our house is the *Pianta e Frammenti della Camera sepolcrale esistenie nella Vigna Casalia Porta S. Sebastiano,* from the *Antichità Romane.* It is a representation of the plan and some fragments from a sepulchral chamber. Piranesi's caption reads:

A: This plan of square form has four grand arches, or apses, today nearly completely covered with earth, which support the walls. They [the arches] are subdivided in other tiny apses, some square and some semicircular, and have a cross-shaped vault finished with compartments of stucco. The building was constructed of square stone tablets, B, and a filling material, C. D: Stairs by which one descends from the columbaria E above to floor A. F: Square niches, or columbaria, each one of which contains two jars, as in the plan G. H: An inscribed pillar with its lid, adorned with an eagle, whose talons grasp the three thunderbolts of Jove. I: The side of the pillar. In this, as in the other opposite, will be seen openings, where there once were rings of iron sealed with lead, with which the ashes were locked up and which were un-covered in the time of the annual libations. K: A cross section of the same item—together with the hole to put the ashes in. L: A sarcophagus of terra cotta, round at one end and flat at the other, with a mound of the same clay serving as a pillow. Not very deep, the same holes mentioned earlier perhaps contained some aro-matic balsam against decay, which also could be introduced from time to time through these apertures, which communicated with the exterior.[3]

This cryptogram underscores Piranesi's fascination with encrypt-ing, a fascination we read in the overt subject matter of his oeuvre: fragments, the unearthed detritus of dead and decaying Rome, obelisks with their in-cised [HIEROGLYPH]s, prisons. This collection of encrypted details, which seep through the frame at one point, corresponds to one of Joyce's telling passages:

But t'[HOUSE] and allaboardshoops! Show coffins, winding sheets, goodbuy bierchepes, cinerary urns, liealoud blasses, snuff-chests, poteentubbs, lacrimal vases, hoodendoses, reekwater-

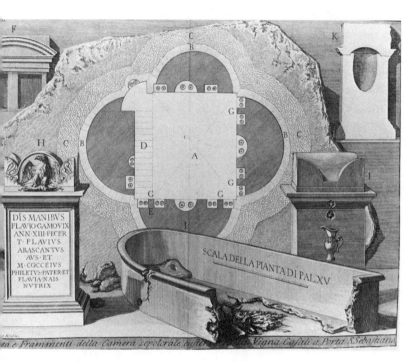

Giovanni Battista Piranesi, *Pianta e Frammenti della Camera sepolcrale esistenie nella Vigna Casali a Porta S. Sebastiano* (ca. 1754)

> beckers, breakmiddles, zootzaks for eatlust, including upyour-
> healthing rookworst and meathewersoftened forkenpootsies and
> for that matter, javel also, any kind of inhumationary bric au brac
> for the adornment of his glasstone honophreum. (*FW*, 77.28–34)

The precious and horrible inventory—"inhumationary bric au brac"—of the
crypt is en(s)crypted in this catalogue of allegorical details.

Here stuff of the past is arranged in decorative fashion to make a
pictorial composition. The title is *"Pianta e Frammenti."* Piranesi has separated the plan from the fragments and given it priority; yet in the etching, the
plan is represented as if it were itself a fragment, apparently inscribed upon a
broken tablet of stone. Thus the plan is both the essential part of the picture—
its necessary, proper, foundational essence—and a part of the collection of
decorative fragments. It shuttles. Furthermore, if we remove the (traditionally) "unnecessary" decorative details from the picture, we have nothing but
a line of etching frame, a line that the details themselves at times push at and
shove. Have they been pushed to the periphery or are they pushing at the
periphery? What is the politics of the frame? There is a shuttling here.

The key to the scale of the etching is inscribed along the interior
wall of the terra cotta sarcophagus. The scale and its container are in perspective. The large plan that serves as a backdrop to the sarcophagus is
orthographic. The four objects in the corners are offered in perspective but
are taken from such a viewpoint as to appear virtually orthographic. The
etching forecasts the death of perspective.

The composition of the four corner objects overlapping the plan
presents them foursquare and "properly" arranged in corners. But the large,
interjecting, phallic sarcophagus moves in from the lower right and veers out
over the lower frame, obstructing part of the captioned title. The word that it
obstructs is *esistenie,* "existing." The sepulchral chamber in which these objects were found is located at the Porta S. Sebastiano. The penetrating form
of the sarcophagus upon the arrangement echoes an emblematicity of its site:
Saint Sebastian, in all his historically depicted passive effeminacy, riddled
with penetrating phallic forms. Body fluids ooze. The holes and channels in
the stone through which liquids flow both in and out provide a reinscription
of the body in the artifacts themselves. These signifiers of the body have nothing to do with symmetry and proportion and even numbers of appendages—
[THE PROPER], classical connectors of the body to architecture.

GAME

Plato said in the *Phaedrus* that "writing can only repeat (itself), that it 'always signifies (*semainei*) the same' and that it is a 'game' (*paidia*)" (quoted in Derrida, *Dissemination*, 65).

Gaming is an important technique of this work, but there is a particular game that appears and reappears, explicitly and implicitly. This is the old, old game called *jeu de l'oie,* the game of goose. Playing this game with my daughter Sarah (who, at four, found it fun and easy to play), I was struck by its complexity. Along with the element of chance, it has a definite structure. A continuous line is interrupted at special points, throwing vectors out to other points, making a weblike construction.

The gameboard of the game of goose is a series of sixty-three numbered squares that wraps around itself in a spiral [BABEL]. One player throws the dice and moves her goose along toward the goal of sixty-three, in the center of the spiral. Along the way are certain squares at which, should a player land on them, special moves are required—stop until another goose comes to the rescue, pass over to another square, pay a penalty. These squares are called the bridge, the well, the inn, the prison, the labyrinth, goose squares, and dead goose. Goose and dead goose require continued linear motion, either toward the goal or back to the starting point. The construction formed by the architectural emblems bridge, well, inn, prison, and labyrinth is a sticky web, an intricate textile in which game players may get caught, a labyrinth superimposed upon the spiral (a dissemination upon an emplotment).

Shortly after my introduction to the game, I happened upon the essay by Michel Serres called "Language and Space: From Oedipus to Zola" in which he names the game of goose as a cultural paradigm that among other things, forms the residue of the *Rougon Macquart* novels by Emile Zola. Serres removes the architectural baggage from the five emblems and sees them as spatial operators, tools for construction. The bridge is a path that connects the disconnected or crosses a fracture. The well is a "hole in space, a local tear in a spatial variety," which both disconnects the connected and connects the disconnected. The inn is a threshold, a relay, an interface; the prison is an enclosed space, a limit. The labyrinth is the total of the other four: "a maze of connection and non-connection, as much closed as it is open, where transport is as much a journey as it is an immobility" (*Hermes,* 42–43).

Here, Serres observes, is the elementary program of topology: connective path, open and closed, tear, continuous and discontinuous, threshold, limit. Here also are the materials by which cultures construct. He writes:

> The fact is that in general a culture constructs in and by its history an original intersection between such spatial varieties, a node of very precise and particular connection. This construction, I believe, is that culture's very history. Cultures are differentiated by the form of the set of junctions, its appearance, its place, as well as by its changes of state, its fluctuations. But what they have in common and what constitutes them as such is the operation itself of joining, of connecting. The image of the weaver arises at this point [WEAVING]: to link, to tie, to open bridges, pathways, wells, or relays among radically different spaces. (*Hermes,* 45)

The game of goose is a map for object-makers, a paradigm for constructions [MAPPING].

HATCHERY

James Joyce has enjoisted a certain construction:

> The boxes, if I may break the subject gently, are worth about fourpence pourbox but I am inventing a more patent process, foolproof and pryperfect (I should like to ask that Shedlock Homes person who is out for removing the roofs of our criminal classics by what *deductio ad domunum* he hopes *de tacto* to detect anything unless he happens of himself, *movibile tectu,* to have a slade off) after which they can be reduced to a fragment of their true crust by even the youngest of Margees if she will take plase to be seated and smile if I please. (*FW,* 165.30–166.2)

This undecidable vessel that commingles eggs, houses, writing, and girls suggests a pseudo-construction we might call a hatchery. Margee is the marginal one, taking her place, seated and smiling, faking, being woman as constituted by the symbolic order. *Movibile tectu,* homophonous to *horribile dictu* ("horrible to tell," unspeakable), refers to a passage from Virgil—repeated throughout the *Aeneid* much as the [HEN]'s [LETTER] is scattered throughout the text of *Finnegans Wake.* And *movibile tectu* is also "moving touch":

the moving finger writes and having writ moves on. Architectural references abound: boxes, Shed, lock (as in locked out of the house), Homes, roofs, classics, domunum, slade.

The hatchery is an apparatus of architecture, writing, and the body. The hatchery is a kind of architectural anti-type; it refers to a kind of built structure (the chicken house), but the structure to which it refers does not belong to the domain of the architect. It is a [HOUSE], but not architecture. Its relation to Laugier's primitive hut is mediated to the point of extreme tentativeness.[4] This is primarily because the form of the hatchery is irrelevant. The hatchery is not bound by theory. It is a para-theoretical device. The hatchery is what is unrepresented when the architecture-making is done. The hatchery is Work in Progress. It is a critical instrument, intrusive and elucidating. It refers to the place where chickens hatch from eggs, source of the life flow, a dirty (soiled) cacaphonous place full of litter, the residue of life (eggshells, excrement, cast-off feathers, uneaten food). In this sense, it is a kind of alchemical [VESSEL], a container of ingredients for the Philosopher's [STONE] (*un vaisseau de pierre*). Its floor is inscribed with the imprints of chicken feet (hatchings and cross-hatchings).

The hatchery is a writing machine. The biddies, the chicks, scratch marks in the dirt. These [HIEROGLYPH]s constitute a historical document, a [MAPPING] and marking of movement. This act of hatching resembles and belongs to the acts of etching, drawing, and writing. It is the act of hatching lines and plots.

The body is, in a sense, a multiply constituted hatchery. It is a messy assemblage of flows—organic, libidinal, synaptic, psychic. The metaphor for the throat—the primary entrance portal—is the hatch, as in "down the hatch." This hatch is a door or passage. We describe our bodies and our constructions in terms of each other, with words as passages between one and the other. Writes of passage, hatcheries all. The hatchery is a bridge between the sacred and the voluptuous, between *physis* and *techne*.

In L. Frank Baum's *Wizard of Oz,* Dorothy's house becomes disconnected at the point of the hatch (trap-door to the cellar underneath) and floats and rises gently in the center of the cyclone. When the house falls, it kills the wicked witch, and Dorothy is construed as a sorceress in a country that is uncivilized and therefore retains a population of sorceresses, witches, and wizards.

Dorothy falls and Alice falls, but into other worlds of magic and strangeness. Adam, Lucifer, Humpty Dumpty, and Icarus fall to less desirable ends. These figures of the construction called masculinity attempt to rise to power and fail, lose, fall from grace. The feminine ones drop out, fall down the hatch, use the exits, find the dreamworld of condensation and displacement, strangeness, and délire. The position to take is perched on the rim of the hole, at the moment the trap door closes, ready to fall. Not to fall from, but *into*. The fall from is hierarchical and you can hurt yourself. The fall into is labyrinthine, dreamy, a dancing fall, a delirious fall.

The hatchery is the domain of Cixous' sorceress: "she makes partial objects circulate." She "uses the exits" (the hatches). "Her rising: is not erection. But diffusion. Not the shaft. The [VESSEL]" (Cixous and Clément, *Newly Born Woman*, 88). The hatchery is both vessel and erection (the topology of erection is vesicular flow, after all), but is neither of these things in the formal sense. Its form must remain indefinite. (The aestheticization of the political is a patriarchal sleight-of-hand power play against which Walter Benjamin warned us long ago.)[5] We can, however, emblematize it with its initial letter. The H is an I in which the shaft has been allowed to rest horizontal for a moment, forming a vessel, a container, a bridge, a conduit.

The hatchery might but cannot be classified into categories. Political, unauthorized and unauthored, it concerns acts, not images; transitory, it is movement, but is not *a* movement. Hacking at the edges of the architecture/state apparatus, it embraces all these categories. It is political and collective and moving.

Barnacles, engulfings, underminings, intrusions: a [MINOR ARCHITECTURE], collective, anonymous, authorless, scratched on the city, the landscape, hatched not birthed. (They are illegitimate—without father.) Bastard constructions. (In some human societies, there is no concept of legitimacy. One is legitimate by virtue of existence. No one knows a single father; many males are the nurturing fathers of all children. Children are born of the mother; they are legitimate by virtue of having made the passage from inside to out.)

"Wee peep[s]" (*FW*, 6.31–32) appear locally upon the landscape of the Gaze. We peeps: we pee, small chicks, brief glances. Tattoos upon the symbolic order. They are the "lens" that "we need the loan of . . . to see as much as the [HEN] saw" (112.1–2). Like minor literature. The little girls on

Tintorelli's stair in *The Trial*. The twenty-eight little-girl shadows of Isabelle, or the rainbow girls in *Finnegans Wake*. Tattoos. T. T. T.'s.

"This battering [BABEL] allower the door and sideposts" (*FW*, 64.9): The hatchery, the place of babes and babble, both allows and lowers the supporting structure of the entrance to the [HOUSE].

[MAPPING]

A biddy architecture: Around midnight. Atlanta, Georgia, 1986. Moving along Techwood Drive, the interstate access road running parallel to I75–85 and accessing the House of Ted Turner. On the right: plantation image, tasteful, white sign with Chippendale frame—"The Turner Broadcasting System." On the left: parallax view of trees silhouetted against the glow of the here submerged interstate highway and, beyond, the city lights. Glimpsed among the trees: small constructions of sticks and draped membranes through which the lights osmose, so strange that you might be hallucinating. Against the membranes, blocking the glow with jarringly recognizable blackness, human figures here and there, existing for the moment between the lines.

Is the hatchery then an architecture?—echoing Julia Kristeva on Philippe Sollers' *H:* "Is *H* then a book?":

> A text that exists only if it can find a reader who matches its
> rhythm—its sentential, biological, corporeal, and trans-familial
> rhythm, infinitely marked out within historical time. . . . "Compo-
> sition instead of happening in the head of an author will happen in
> nature and real space with consequently immense objective wealth
> in addition impeding underhanded appropriation necessitating
> the risks of execution" [Sollers]. (*Desire in Language*, 207)

The hatchery is an assemblage. It is what you cannot see when the making is done. It is not a metaphor; it cannot be reified. Deleuze and Guattari: "Assemblages are passional, they are compositions of desire. Desire has nothing to do with a natural or spontaneous determination; there is no desire but assembling, assembled, desire. The rationality, the efficiency, of an assemblage does not exist without the passions the assemblage brings into play, without the desires that constitute it as much as it constitutes them" (*Thousand Plateaus*, 399).

HEN

The hen (the biddy, the mother, Annalivia) in *Finnegans Wake* is both the writer of the [LETTER] and the reader—the raider (it is the hen who scratches up all the excremental bits of the consumed, digested, and excreted letter from the midden heap), of the letter. The raiding, or rewriting, is accomplished by scratching in the dumping ground.

"A text is not a text unless it hides from the first comer, from the first glance, the law of its composition and the rules of its game" (*Dissemination,* 63). This first sentence of Derrida's "Plato's Pharmacy" follows a heading, a dictionary entry on *kolaphos,* that is the last word of Littré's definition of *coup* (the last word of Derrida's previous chapter). This heading is a joint between Derrida's construction and mine. Emerging out of *coup* ("a blow"; *un coup d'oeil,* "a glance or gaze," literally, "a blow of the eye"; the sound of certain birds—pigeon coup),[6] the *kolaphos* entry prefigures Derrida's text, in which is hidden an other text. In the pecking of birds, the horse's hoof striking the ground (the Trojan [GAME]), inscription, engraving, to scratch, and Gluph, in these [HIEROGLYPH]s, we can decipher the name of the en(s)crypted text: *Finnegans Wake.*

A footnote in "Plato's Pharmacy" is to the point. It occurs in a passage in which the text slides among relations of Thoth (Th'other), the god of writing and the son of the sun, Ammon-Ra (whose name when pronounced sounds like the Egyptian word meaning "to hide"); Ammon Ra himself; the world; the egg; and the bird in whose form Ammon Ra appears. The passage demarcates a vague container that both holds the hidden content of the hieroglyph (bird) of Ra (the "other" of writing), and displays the (more apparent) power of speech. The note is embedded in the text adjacent to the words *hidden egg* (87–88) and includes an ambiguous statement, "the whole of this essay being nothing more than a reading of *Finnegans Wake,* as the reader will quickly have realized."[7]

HIEROGLYPH

In the British Museum and Library in London, on any given day, lie, within a few hundred feet of each other, the Rosetta [STONE] and the hundreds of sheets of many different kinds and sizes of paper, from proper writing paper to café menus, scrawled in many pencil and ink colors and layers, and organized in several archival boxes, that comprise Joyce's manuscript for *Finnegans Wake*. In fact, the patient search through Joyce's chicken scratch for evidence of geometry and pattern (the beginnings of architecture) was not unlike (I imagined) the labor of Thomas Young and Jean François Champollion, who, in series, deciphered the writing on the black slab found at Rosetta in 1799.

On this armload of basalt, which looks very much like any of several irregularly shaped tables of stone inscribed with figures in the etchings of Piranesi, are carved sections of text that are clearly three forms of writing. One section is Greek; the other two Egyptian: one in a cursive form, the other in picture writing. These pictures are *hieroglyphs,* "sacred carvings." Before the Rosetta Stone was discovered, hieroglyphic writing was illegible to any living human being on the planet. It could not be read; it did not make any sense. There were many theories about what it meant and how it meant: in other words, people understood that it was an instrument of representation, but they could not figure out a workable relation between hieroglyph and representation. But in the hieroglyphic text of the Rosetta Stone is a cartouche that is repeated six times throughout the text. Early on, Young identified this cartouche, a figure framed by an oval incision, as the name of Ptolemy. From this system of initial clue, he began; and then Champollion, a young man who by the age of sixteen had mastered eight ancient languages, deciphered the collection of incised voids that, for hundreds of years, had been thoroughly illegible, yet had accrued a great body of significance. Without being attached to words, hieroglyphs still carried connotations.

The undecidable meanings that undeciphered hieroglyphs convey and that architecture, another form of illegible script, conveys, are approached by Roland Barthes:

> Now it happens that in this country (Japan) the empire of sig-
> nifiers is so immense, so in excess of speech, that the exchange
> of signs remains of a fascinating richness, mobility, and sub-
> tlety, despite the opacity of the language, sometimes even as a
> consequence of that opacity. The reason for this is that in Japan
> the body exists, acts, shows itself, gives itself, without hysteria,
> without narcissism, but according to a pure—though subtly dis-
> continuous—erotic project. It is not the voice (with which we
> identify the "rights" of the person) which communicates . . . ,

but the whole body (eyes, smile, hair, gestures, clothing) which
sustains with you a sort of babble that the perfect domination
of the codes strips of all regressive, infantile character. To make
a date . . . may take an hour, but during that hour, . . . it is the
other's entire body which has been known, savored, received, and
which has displayed (to no real purpose) its own narrative, its
own text. (*Empire of Signs*, 9–10)

HOUSE

Language begins in caves (Vico). Art begins in caves (Bataille). But
architecture begins with the primitive hut (Laugier).

In the Garden of Eden there was no architecture. The necessity for
architecture arose with the ordination of sin and shame, with dirty bodies.
The fig leaf was a natural first impulse toward architecture, accustomed as it
was to shading its grotesque fruit. Was it the fig tree that was hacked up to
build the primitive hut?

Western architecture is, by its nature, a phallocentric discourse,
containing, ordering, and representing through firmness, commodity, and
beauty: consisting of orders, entablature, and architrave; base, shaft, and
capital; nave, choir, and apse; father, son, and spirit, world without end
amen.

The primitive hut and all its begettings constitute a house of many
mansions, a firm, commodious, and beautiful erection. This is the house of
my fathers. But there is the beginning of an intrusive presence in this house.

It is hard to disagree with Audre Lorde's much-cited dictum that
the Master's tools will never dismantle the Master's house. But
people have to live in a house, not in a metaphor. Of *course* you
use the Master's tools if those are the only ones you can lay your
hands on. Perhaps what you can do with them is to take apart that
old mansion, using some of its pieces to put up a far better one
where there is room for all of us. (Robinson, "Canon Fathers, 34)[8]

HYSTERICAL DOCUMENTS

The problem is that you can't talk about your private life in the
course of doing your professional work. You have to pretend that
epistemology, or whatever you're writing about, has nothing to

do with your life, that it's more exalted, more important, because it (supposedly) transcends the merely personal. Well, I'm tired of the conventions that keep discussions of epistemology, or James Joyce, segregated from meditations on what is happening outside my window or inside my heart. The public-private dichotomy, which is to say, the public-private hierarchy, is a founding condition of female oppression. I say to hell with it. The reason I feel embarrassed at my own attempts to speak personally in a professional context is that I have been conditioned to feel that way. That's all there is to it. (Tompkins, "Me and My Shadow," 122–123)

D'occupant	Term
Sarah Elizabeth	8 April 1979 until 15 January 1980
Unnamed child	2 February until 4 March 1984
Unnamed child	March 1990 until 13 May 1990
Laura Barrett	15 July 1990 until 8 April 1991

INTERVAL

"The hysteric . . . is between the family walls, which she does not leave, and a *jeune naissance,* the I-nnascence that is not yet accomplished" (Clément, in Cixous and Clément, *Newly Born Woman,* 55).

1 a: a space of time between the recurrences of similar conditions or states . . . 2 a: a space between things . . .3 : something that breaks or interrupts a uniform series or surface . . .4 *chiefly New Eng[land]:* BOTTOM [low lying land, especially that near a river] (*Webster's Third International Dictionary*)

An interval is a connection, an intervention, a hole in the wall, a space of incision, a place of alluvial soil. It is the space between the walls proper, the space of the joint.

This fissure is not one among others. It is the fissure: the necessity of interval, the harsh law of spacing. It could not endanger song except by being inscribed in it from its birth and in its essence. Spacing is not the accident of song. . . . In the *Dictionary,* the interval is a part of the definition of song. It is therefore, so to speak, an originary accessory and an essential accident. Like writing. (Derrida, *Grammatology,* 200)

LETTER

"The letter! The litter! And the soother the bitther! Of eyebrow pencilled, by lipstipple penned" (*FW*, 93.24–25).

The letter, written by a [HEN], pecked up and excreted (hidden) in a midden heap, where, in order to (re)construct it, one must dig through all the soil to find the many little bits, is an analogue of writing as an act of resistance, writing the unspeakable, the secret(ed).

The letter also relates to analysis and has particular connections to psychoanalysis. At this point the hen's letter and Poe's "Purloined Letter," with all of its subsequent textuality, intersect.[9] Within fourteen lines, Joyce skims the psychoanalytic territory of the purloined letter: "Theodicy *re*'furloined notepaper . . . is a pinch of scribble, not wortha bottle of cabbis. Overdrawn!" (419.30–33). "Flummery is what I would call . . . them bagses of trash which the mother and Mr Unmentionable (O breed not his same!) has reduced to writing without making news out of my sootynemm. When she slipped under her couchman. And where he made a cat with a peep" (420.1–7).

The hen's letter, now masquerading as "The Purloined Letter," is a piece of overdrawn (both scratched over [*hachée*] and divested of content) flummery ("something poor, trashy, or not worth having . . . foolish, deceptive language") constructed by the mother and a couchman, "Mr Unmentionable." One "couchman" who "made a cat with a peep" is named Sigmund Freud. Recall his boast, *"J'appelle un chat un chat"* (I call a pussy a pussy), made in reference to his insistence upon calling "unmentionable" body parts by their proper names when around a female patient. Many following Freud have noticed his own slip: he unironically uses French slang— the surrounding text is German—to convey the word *vulva*. This is a classic "purloined letter," in a double sense: first, his subtext hangs out in the open for all to see and, second, the purloined letter stands in for in the post-Lacanian discourse about it—what woman lacks, the site of the discovery of this, and the abyssal machinations of lack-as-castration, lack-as-castration-as-truth, the truth of lack-as-castration-as-truth, and so forth, generated by the story itself via Lacan and his followers.

In all of this plotting, "The Purloined Letter" itself becomes a purloined letter à la Lacan, that is, it is "able to produce its effects within the story: on the actors in the tale, including the narrator, as well as outside the story: on us, the readers, and also on its author, without anyone's ever bothering to worry about what it meant" ("Seminar," 57). The power of the purloined letter lies not in what it means, but in how it works. Barbara Johnson adds, " 'The Purloined Letter' thus becomes for Lacan a kind of allegory of the signifier" ("Frame of Reference," 464). In the translation of Jeffrey Mehlman (of whose postman-like name Derrida has already made much in the final pages of *Carte Postale*), Lacan further explains:

> Just so does the purloined letter, like an immense female body, stretch out across the Minister's office when Dupin enters. But just so does he already expect to find it. . . . And that is why without needing any more than being able to listen in at the door of Professor Freud, he will go straight to the spot in which lies and lives what that body is designed to hide, in a gorgeous center caught in a glimpse, nay, to the very place seducers name Sant'Angelo's Castle in their innocent illusion of controlling the City from within it. Look! between the cheeks of the fireplace, there's the object already in reach of a hand the ravisher has but to extend. ("Seminar," 66–67)

The Castello Sant'Angelo, that great, red, O-shaped, fortress-ruin by the Tiber, appears frequently in the etchings of Piranesi.[10] The inventions for which he was perhaps best known are his designs for fireplaces. Like the *Carceri*, and other inventions of Piranesi, they might be considered "Overdrawn."

Other Letters

Most of us—those of us who are women; to those who are men this will not apply—probably check the *F* box rather than the *M* box when filling out an application form. It would hardly occur to us to mark *M*. It would be like cheating or, worse, not existing, like erasing ourselves from the world. (For men to check the *F* box, were they ever tempted to do so, would have quite another set of implications.) For since the very first time we put a check mark on the little square next to the *F* on the form, we have officially become en-gendered as women; that is to say, not only do other people consider us females, but from that moment on we have been representing ourselves as women. Now, I ask, isn't that the same as saying that the *F* next to the little box, which we marked in filling out the form, has stuck to us like a wet, silk dress? Or that while we thought that we were marking the *F* on the form, in fact the *F* was marking itself on us? (de Lauretis, *Technologies of Gender*, 11–12)

The letter is also the person who lets: lets go, lets fly, lets loose. And it is a form of this letting—the letter is of the "personal" "where writing, freed from law, unencumbered by moderation, exceeds phallic authority, and where the subjectivity inscribing its effects becomes feminine [regardless of gender]" (Cixous, in Cixous and Clément, *Newly Born Woman*, 86).

9 August, 1987
Nagasaki
Dear Jennifer:

Are you the true discoverer of JJ's use of Soane? It is convincing. And your paper is exemplary and fun to read. Do you know John Gordon's "FW: A Plot Summary"? A revelation. The whole book happens in a room in Chapelizod. The guided tour of the Museyroom is an inventory of the room, based on a mnemonic device of sharpening your memory by rehearsing all the objects in a room you know well. (Not till summer before last did I finally track down and read Sheridan Lefanu's "The House by the Churchyard," ALL of which is worked into the Wake. Even Anna Liffey. The plot is labyrinthine, but the nub is that a man unconscious from a blow must be trepanned, in the hope that he will, before dying, say who slew him. His rebirth is unavoidably his death.) . . .

Broiling here, too. I've just noticed your home address. Will try it, next letter. What's the dissertation on? I'm just beginning to read Tony Vidler's new book, discovering that he's already told me the good parts (about Fourier).
Bless you . . . ,
Guy[11]

And a Postcard:

5 July, 1988

Cambridge

Dear Peter,

Dans la région où s'érige le désir sans contrainte, la raison du plus fort n'est pas toujours meilleur. You see the limit of my interest.

Yours,

Jennifer

P.S. Did you find my umbrellas? [12]

"The letter as a signifier is thus not a thing or the absence of a thing, nor a word or the absence of a word, nor an organ or the absence of an organ, but a *knot* in a structure where words, things and organs can neither be definably separated nor compatibly combined" (Johnson, "Frame of Reference, 498).

MAPPING

The landscape may be patterned by the lines of movement. In the case of the Arunta in Australia the entire territory is magically organized by a network of mythical paths linking together a series of isolated totemic "countries" or clan estates, and leaving waste areas between. There is normally only one correct trail to the sacred storehouse containing totemic objects, and [Olive] Pink tells of the long detour made by one of his guides to approach a sacred place properly.

[Pierre] Jaccard speaks of a famous Arab guide in the Sahara, who could follow the faintest trail, and for whom the entire desert was a network of paths. In one instance he followed painstakingly the continuous twists of the scarcely-marked way, even while his destination was clearly visible to him across the open desert. This reliance was habitual, since storms and mirages often made distant landmarks unreliable. Another author writes of the Saharan *Medjbed,* the transcontinental path worn by camels that goes for hundreds of kilometers over the empty land from water hole to water hole, marked by piles of stones at crossing points. It may mean death to lose it. He speaks of the strong personality, the almost sacred character, that this trace acquires. In quite another landscape, the seemingly impenetrable African forest, the tangle is intersected by elephant paths, which natives learn and traverse as we might learn and traverse city streets. (Lynch, *Image of the City*, 130)

Piranesi's "systematic criticism of the concept of place" and Joyce's systematic criticism of the concept of history are carried out through "all this breaking up, distorting, multiplying, and disarranging" (Tafuri, *Sphere and Labyrinth*, 27). Theirs is a recasting of interpretation that rejects the transcendence, directness, and authority embodied in "place" and "history," a recasting carried out by processes that can perhaps best be described as mapping.

Compare Piranesi's *Collegio* drawing to the landscape described above. In each case, there is a "rational" interpretation: in the desert, [THE PROPER] way to go between here and there—we can *see* it—is a straight line; in the drawing, we *see* a baroque plan that valorizes the concept of center. But in both cases, to another tracker the details are signs of much more going on, an erasure of the authority of line, a bulls-eye critique of the concept of center. The beautifully composed and apparently contained *Collegio*

is in fact a structure theoretically endlessly expandable. The independence of the parts and their montage obey no other law than that of pure *contiguity*. The *Collegio*, then, constitutes a kind of gigantic question mark on the meaning of architectural composition: the "clarity" of the planimetric choice is subtly eroded by the process with which the various parts engage in mutual dialogue; the single space secretly undermines the laws to which it pretends to subject itself. (Tafuri, *Sphere and Labyrinth*, 31)

If we pay attention to the details and the detours, we will go much farther.

—There has to be somewhere else, I tell myself. And everyone knows that to go somewhere there are routes, signs, "maps"—for an exploration, a trip.

—That's what books are. Everyone knows that a place exists which is not economically or politically indebted to all the vileness and compromise. That is not obliged to reproduce the system. That is writing. If there is a somewhere else that can escape the infernal repetition, it lies in that direction, where *it* writes itself, where *it* dreams, where *it* invents new worlds. (Cixous, in Cixous and Clément, *Newly Born Woman*, 72)

P.S. *Un chateau des cartes* is also a house of maps.

MINOR ARCHITECTURE

The concept of minor architecture is both properly deduced from Manfredo Tafuri's concept of "major architecture" and illegitimately appropriated from Gilles Deleuze and Felix Guattari's concept of minor literature. Minor literature is writing that takes on the conventions of a major language in order to subvert it from the inside. Deleuze and Guattari study the work of Franz Kafka, a Jew writing in German in Prague during the early part of this century. Minor literature possesses three dominant characteristics:

· It is what a minority constructs within a major language, deterritorializing that language. Deleuze and Guattari compare Prague German to Black American English.

· It is intensely political: "Its cramped space forces each individual intrigue to connect immediately to politics. The individual concern thus becomes all the more necessary, indispensable, magnified because a whole other story is vibrating within it" (*Kafka*, 17). In other words, in minor literature the distinction between personal and political dissolves.

· It is a collective assemblage; everything in it takes on a collective value.

Deleuze and Guattari describe two paths of deterritorialization. One is to "artificially enrich [the language], to swell it up through all the resources of symbolism, of oneirism, of esoteric sense, of a hidden signifier." This is a Joycean approach. The other is to take on the poverty of a language and take it farther, "to the point of sobriety" (*Kafka*, 19). This is Kafka's way. Deleuze and Guattari then reject the Joycean as a kind of closet reterritorialization that breaks from the people, and they go all the way with Kafka.

In transferring such a concept to architecture, already more intensely simple materially, and with more complex connections to "the people" and to pragmatics, I believe it necessary to hang onto both possibilities, shuttling between them. This may begin to delineate a line of scrimmage between making architectural objects and writing architectonic texts.

A minor architecture should embrace a collection of practices that follow these conditions. One of the tasks of minor architecture is to operate critically upon the dominance of the visual—the image—as a mode of perceiving and understanding architecture. Thus, what a work of minor architecture looks like is irrelevant outside of the condition of its "looking like" architecture. I do not, therefore, propose a style or an *architecture parlante* but a revolutionary architectural criticism, a "criticism from within" that goes deeply into the within, into the conventions of architecture's collusion with mechanisms of power. (These may possibly include every architectural convention.)

John Hejduk was making these kinds of moves over a decade ago. "Bye, House" (to misread) connotes not simply the house and its owner, but a farewell to the object as traditionally constituted, an involution, a [HOUSE] turned inside out, one in which the [CRYPT]s within the walls explode, protrude, seep, bleed out from within to become without. And in which the skin, which was without, which named the image House, has shriveled and become compacted into a dense, Euclidean plane from which the partial objects protrude and against which they are projected. Here, Hejduk has consumed Le Corbusier and Colin Rowe (his fathers) in a single gulp, and has excreted (evacuated, voided) them as the assemblage named Bye House.

In 1988, Hejduk's House of the Suicide and House of the Mother of the Suicide were encrypted in the architecture building at the Georgia Institute of Technology, crippled by indecisive (unfunded) incompleteness for years. This condition of incompletion was testimony to the ability of the profession to lock up the house and swallow the key. But these incomplete objects were further marginalized: they remained to stick in the craw, consumed but not digested, irritating the system. They were always there, partial and worrisome. Mute and flayed, and without their overtly threatening frozen Medusan fright wigs, they were perhaps more prickly and threatening to the Big House than they are now that they are complete, finished, and beautifully detailed. There they continue to sit, however, and in 1992 the taste of systemic irritation remains.

The incomplete project defies authority. The House of my Fathers is a valid (repeatable, contained, complete) project. The incomplete house is invalid, a sick body in the system, an uncomfortable blockage of the system's ability to consume what threatens.

MIRROR

How can I deal with the mirror, that wonder-ful metaphor of truthful representation. The world held in a surface of undiffused light. Virtual reality, virtual image. It isn't really there at all. A mirage. Fata morgana. Laura Barrett sees Baby-in-the-Mirror and wiggles and laughs and reaches out for her, calling, "baba, baba!" Sarah at twelve stands transfixed before the mirror, seeking the woman she thinks/knows/hopes/fears? she is becoming. At forty, I see the woman in the mirror receding from me; less and less am I defined by her. I am letting her go. Which, if any, of us sees a "truthful representation"? If the "real thing" does not quite work, why should the metaphor?

"I ask you to refuse what I offer because that is not it" (Jacques Lacan, *Encore*, 114).

PATCHWORK

Sewing/"sewering"/dissemination, collectivity, piecework, the feminine, raggedy, of rags, (of rage), related to [WEAVING] (the poetic), stains of pricks/blood and bleeding, the prick of the shuttle in "Sleeping Beauty" [ROCKET], eye patch, patching holes, garden patch, working a little bit of something.

> Patchwork, for its part, may display equivalents to themes, symmetries, and resonance that approximate it to embroidery. But the fact remains that its space is not at all constituted in the same way: there is no center; its basic motif ("block") is composed of a single element; the recurrence of this element frees uniquely rhythmic values distinct from the harmonies of embroidery (in particular, in "crazy" patchwork, which fits together pieces of varying size, shape, and color, and plays on the *texture* of the fabrics.) (Deleuze and Guattari, *Thousand Plateaus*, 476)

The patchwork quilt is an American artifact, originating in scarcity, in lack. The knowledge informing its making is traditionally passed one to one, in conversation and demonstration, mother to daughter. A quilt is constructed from scraps and bits of material from many different sources selected both to function well together (in terms of thermal comfort and washability) and to create a pleasing and significant pattern. Like a wall, the quilt is assembled of layers of various material, each with its own function, fastened together. Assembling the layers—quilting—is often a collective enterprise, a bee, a gathering of many individuals to contribute to the completion of one individual's project: gifts of time and self. Often a quilt is constructed as a gift, usually for a new bride or a new baby, and sometimes, as with the AIDS quilt, for those who are living so that we may remember the dead. Over a collection of quilts within a community may be mapped an intricate network of gift exchange [MAPPING]. Quilts are made by human beings working together—making, talking, touching. Both inscription and construction, the quilt possesses a spatiality beyond the immediate.

The conventions of patchwork are strong: there are typologies of pattern, proprieties of stitching method and length, ancient rules of thumb. It contains "striation": those "proper" tiny stitches of great uniformity forced by the tyranny of grandmother or mother [THE PROPER]. The crazy quilt is an exquisite model of invention under conditions of scarcity. It relies on the fabrication of joints among scraps of preexisting (leftover) shapes.[13] Here, theory as authority fades to the dominance of pragmatics and invention. By *pragmatics,* I suggest not only such categories as material and function, but also the important category of use, which includes the quilt's role as a historical project, a memory construct: here is a bit of last year's Easter dress, this piece from grandmother's curtains (which brings to mind the doll's dress also made from them), this from another outworn quilt we used to take naps on under the apple tree in the back yard, there a piece of our old everyday tablecloth. A slice of family history that is not about lines of legitimacy and trees, the patchwork quilt is a construction that signifies the pale, faint layers of otherness that lie within the dominant.

In Riemannian (non-Euclidean, Joycean, Piranesian) space, " 'Each vicinity is therefore like a shred of Euclidean space, but the linkage between one vicinity and the next is not defined and can be effected in an infinite number of ways. Riemann space at its most general thus presents itself as an amorphous collection of pieces that are juxtaposed but not attached to each other.' . . . In short, if we follow Lautmann's fine description [just quoted], Riemannian space is pure patchwork" (Deleuze and Guattari, *Thousand Plateaus,* 485).

PHARMAKON

Plato (in the *Phaedrus*) first draws us into the question of writing as a pharmakon—a drug or potion that is both a poison and a cure—when he asks whether writing is a good thing or a bad thing. The question of whether writing is a benign, faithful reflection of speech or a diabolical [VESSEL], with "Truth" on the label but leaking belying contaminants, has appeared here and there in print ever since. In twentieth-century discourse around this question, the [HIEROGLYPH] figures prominently. All the paters whose names and work appear in this construction, especially Walter B., Peter, and the Jacks, work with and around this place between writing and drawing.

In a letter to "Jack Derippa," in care of "Abroad," Michael Phillipson as Ethelred Ameurunculus writes of approaching the Sibyl with a thirteen-page question, no part of which I can reproduce here without permission in writing from the publishers. The question involves the doubled and doubling nature of writing (both Jim and Jack are named as exemplars or culprits), and suggests writing's desire to draw, in the sense of leading or pulling someone somewhere, but also in the sense of that other possibility of the word that has to do with black marks made by architects on paper. Curiously, fabulously, the Sibyl answers the question in a long collage-poem constructed of lines from children's nursery rhymes (see *Modernity's Wake,* 142–157). "Sperm, water, ink, paint, perfumed dye: the pharmakon always penetrates like a liquid; it is absorbed, drunk, introduced into the inside, which it first marks with the hardness of the type, soon to invade it and inundate it with its medicine, its brew, its drink, its potion, its poison" (Derrida, *Dissemination,* 152).

POCHE

The word *poché* is a past participle of the French *pocher,* "to blacken." (It also means "to poach," as in egg; "to dash off," as in a rough sketch or essay; and "to make baggy at the knees," as in a pair of trousers.) It is a relative of *poche,* "a pocket or pouch," "a pucker," or—"a sinkhole"

[VESSEL]. *Une pochette* is a handbag, and *une pochetée* is "a pocketful," or a stupid person. In architectural drawings (sections and plans), poché is the representation of solid material that has been cut through—walls, columns, and beams, for example. In the representation, the space within the outline of the element being sectioned is blackened. Occasionally, an element that may appear in a "real" building to be solid actually contains a pocket within it; sometimes, this poche, an [INTERVAL], constitutes a hidden, secret room represented as a white void within the poché of the drawing of the building.

During my middle childhood, I lived in a coalmining town in southwest Virginia. One of my most distinct memories is the sight of the miners, covered with blackness, emerging from those great holes in the earth. Their faces, lined and tired and smudged with a greasy black that gave their blue eyes (eyes that wrote large their generations-of-Scotch-Irish-immigrants-up-in-the-hills heritage) an almost inhuman aspect. The coal dust was everywhere; at the end of each day, mothers poked white washcloths up the noses of their children. The washcloths came out with black circles on them.

My best friends, in this time before boys had to be dealt with seriously, were twin boys who lived on the same ridge as my family. They lived in a new, brick house. Upstairs, accessible through a hole in the back of the closet of one of the bedrooms, was a tiny "secret" room, perhaps four feet by six feet by four feet high. In there, we kept flashlights and books, lots of books, and there, Shem and Shaun and I fed our other-world desiring on many rainy afternoons. It was a thrilling place. Shem, who went on to Ivy League schools and a brilliant career, died recently from a dark, dark virus, having spent his life hiding secrets inside himself.

Recently, I did some architectural work for an organization that works to hide and protect women and their children who have escaped homes in which they have been terrorized by men who think that they love them. This "shelter" is in a secret place, nestled in a pocket cleared within a tangle of lush, dark, Florida foliage. In beginning to think about the design, I went regularly to weekly meetings of women who had contacted the shelter for help, and who were gathering the courage to leave their homes. In my naïveté, I was astounded at who these women were. They included everyone: a woman with knife-wound scars way up on her thighs where they would not show, who was reluctant to leave her stable of horses and to take her children out of their private school; an angry, overweight woman with ill-fitting, ill-matched clothes; loud, assertive women; soft-spoken, frightened women; black women; white women; Latinas; students; unemployed women; professional women. One woman was married to a police chief, another to a minister. It is tempting here to work the metaphor of black eyes, dark bruises, and the small round pits of scars made by burning cigarettes into this text on poché. But these were not metaphors; they were real. One night, a girl of perhaps fourteen spoke of her hiding place, reached through a hole in the back of her closet, a place where she felt safe from her father, who frequently used her to satisfy his sexual desires.

In the convention of architectural drawing, poché is effected by hatch marks, a kind of chicken scratch, made with a drawing instrument across the paper [HATCHERY, HEN]. Poché offers blackness, obscurity, dark pockets in a properly ordered world [THE PROPER], safe and comforting places, places where things people are afraid to voice openly can be hidden. Places of umbrage.

THE PROPER

"That inharmonious detail, did you name it?" This is Joyce, referring to "a selfraising syringe and twin feeders (you know . . . as well as I do (and don't try to hide it) the penals lots I am now poking at) (*FW*, 188.26–32).

The words *proper, property,* and *propriety* come to us from the Latin *proprius,* meaning "one's own," "special," "particular." The adverb, *proprie,* means "exclusively for oneself." The proper name is the founding condition of that which is proper. The removal of a slave's or wife's proper name and the substitution of another proper name or giving one's proper name to one's child are acts of marking that person as one's own, or exclusively for oneself.

The proper is the emblematic mantra of our (and others') culture. By means of an anagram game, we can reveal what is hidden in the proper: pop, pope, rope, prop, and ero ("I will"). But there is also a pore.

In an essay in which she uses structural failure in architecture as a trope for the failure of the world of the proper to shelter properly the "babbling King" in Shakespeare's play *King Lear* and then reverses the direction of the trope to speak to architecture, Catherine Ingraham points to this hole, this beginning of fissure, of fault.

Lear's exposure of a certain relation of the proper—in the Derridean sense of that which inaugurates the crisis of self-identity—to property . . . reveals a new territory that . . . gives the dangerous illusion of shelter but "lets the weather in." Under this leaky roof . . . are built the mythical structures that we call kingdoms, cities, homes, or, more philosophically, the structures of the proper, the proper name, self-consciousness that is at home with itself. When the faultlines that break up shelter are revealed . . . not as exceptional fissures . . . but as part of the ordinary and everyday banalities of house and home, then, to put it mildly, all hell breaks loose. . . . One might say that architecture comes into its own the moment the structure of the proper is destabilized. For it is at this moment that the real ground is broken and form is given. ("Faults of Architecture," 12)

ROCKET

The rocket is an ambiguous emblem. On the surface, it is a phallic instrument of hyper-colonization and weaponry. It exudes a "red glare." But the rocket comes to us from the *rochetto,* an instrument of textile-making, which shuttles back and forth, always in ex-stasis. *Rochetto* is the diminutive of *rocca,* "a distaff." In English, the distaff, a staff with a slot in one end used in spinning, is a metonymy for woman. In genealogy, we refer to the maternal branch as the "distaff side." (The paternal branch is known as the "spear side.")

Woman is excessive, ex-orbitant (outside the orbit—of the rocket's satellite, of the eye). Woman as architect is ultra-exorbitant: recall the constructions that Daedalus made. Gesture, as of the hand, and gestation, as of the container [VESSEL], share a logical ancestor. So, where does she go, having run out of the [HOUSE] of her fathers and been locked out of the house of radicality? She goes to secret places between the walls [POCHE], exorbitant spaces. She goes out of the orbit of the status quo, and draws her way back in along the orbit lines. She, like most women, people of color, gays and lesbians, and others feared and therefore oppressed, shuttles back and forth between the house proper and the hiding places within. Shuttling, like mediation (see chapter 1), prepares the way for the dissolution of bipolarities; it deterritorializes.

But here I have jabbed my own heel. How can I, a white, bourgeois, academic woman, sitting smack as a woman can in the center, presume to identify with those in the margins? The other side of the question, and the answer, is, How can I not?

Gayatri Spivak approaches this problematic:

The putative center welcomes selective inhabitants of the margin in order better to exclude the margin. And it is the center that offers the official explanation; or, the center is defined and re-produced by the explanation that it can express. . . . By pointing attention to a feminist marginality, I have been attempting, not to win the center for ourselves, but to point at the irreducibility of the margin in all explanations. That would not merely reverse but displace the distinction between margin and center. But in effect such pure innocence (pushing all guilt to the margins) is not possible, and, paradoxically, would put the very law of displacement and the irreducibility of the margin into question. The only way I can hope to suggest how the center itself is marginal is by not remaining outside in the margin and pointing my accusing finger at the center. I might do it rather by implicating myself in that center and sensing what politics make it marginal. Since one's vote is at the limit for oneself, the deconstructivist can use herself (assuming one is at one's own disposal) as a shuttle between the center (inside) and the margin (outside) and thus narrate a displacement. (*Other Worlds,* 107)

bell hooks points an accurate finger at white academics who construct discourses of alterity with the professed purpose of eradicating racism while sitting comfortably within institutions that perpetuate racial domination. Her prescription is another form of shuttling: "One change in direction that would be real cool would be the production of a discourse on race that interrogates whiteness. It would just be so interesting for all those white folks who are giving blacks their take on blackness to let them know what's going on with whiteness" (*Yearning,* 54).

Such shuttling activity declines to define limits, new or old; it puts them back into circulation—properly.

STONE

The tradition of architecture is stone-piling. Architecture was for a long time made by piling stone upon stone, each having been properly cut and fitted, to assemble predetermined, orderly buildings [HOUSE, THE PROPER]. The stonework in this construction is more in the realm of a three-dimensional mosaic—a construction of stones (words: recall Nietzsche's metaphor) and stony motifs that provide one layer of an architecturally emplotted armature.

A map of the construction of stones (*un vaisseau de pierre*) would include the following networks of itineraries [MAPPING]:

Campo Marzio mapped on stone

Ten Commandments graven in stone   Rosetta Stone

Rock of Ages   Rocket (rochetta)   Osiris' stone penis

stone obelisk with glyphs   Lacan's stone phallus

Phoenix Park stone (penis of HCE)   family jewels

pierre   pietra   Peter   one-eyed trouser snake

Medusa's evil eye   Cyclops   cyclopean masonry

stony sediment   river stones   dumping ground

mosaics   Cheval's Palace   Pynchon's Bad Priest

rolling stone   Sisyphus   wandering jew-els

Nietzsche's rock rising from the sea

rolling away the stone

Shem and Shaun (stem and stone)

Benjamin's petrified landscape

foundations of stone

theory   cornerstone   tablets of stone

a stone's throw   stone weight   calculus

game of Go (smooth space of Deleuze and Guattari)

UNDESIRABLE BEASTS

Beast is defined as "any animal except man." In this use of *man*, the term refers to both genders and all races of the human species. Yet if we take a look at the art, literature, and slang of Western culture, we might find the definition less inclusive. In our culture, women, blacks, and other others are identified with all kinds of beasts: serpents, bucks, cows, cats and kittens, dogs and bitches, hens and chicks, and bunnies, to name a few. Beasts are for production and reproduction, not reason. Beastliness is not proper, and beasts have no property rights [THE PROPER]. Beasts crawl and creep and roam throughout this document. There are spiders, chickens, moles, geese, horses, cows, lice, and more.

WEAVING

My loom has sat virtually untouched, except for an occasional loving dusting, since this book-that-was-a-dissertation began. It now displays an ancient, sagging warp that, when I put it on those many years ago, was tight and even as a belly eight months pregnant. Woven among the threads of the warp as "trash" (junky stuff that a weaver first puts into her piece to adjust the tension and width) are several strips of the newsprint tabloid in which my first article was published (the words *Piranesi, Joyce,* and *architecture* appear, partial but recognizable, on the yellowed, brittle newsprint snaking its way among the cotton threads) and then a few dozen throws of the shuttle with the sensuous, lanolin-laden gray wool that comes from the black sheep. It is as if I knew that this beginning would be with me for a long time and therefore used meaningful and beautiful material as trash. The tissue that it makes is both strange and familiar, a memory device that calls up the dot-to-dot picture that is the continuity of domestic life (meals, friends, quarrels, dances, growing children), an emplotment upon which the constellation of professional life (lectures, students, airplanes, reviews, growing debate) has been disseminated. The histology of this tissue (a word that comes from the same root as *text* and the *-tecture* of *architecture*) is jarringly familiar.

> Hist- *or* histo- *comb form* [F, fr. Gk *histos* mast, beam of a loom, loom, web, fr. *histanai* to cause to stand . . .]: tissue (*Websters Third International Dictionary*)

A tissue is a textured weaving. The metaphors—historical tissue, literary tissue, sociological tissue, and urban tissue—are commonly used in thinking about the institutions or objects named in them. In histological analysis, tissues are subjected to very thin slicing (they are sectioned [POCHE]), and in the residual section, we can see traces of the internecine structures of interlacing threads that go off in different directions and tie themselves back together with other threads.

"We will keep within the limits of this tissue: between the metaphor of the histos and the question of the histos of metaphor" (Derrida, *Dissemination*, 65).

One of the dominant conventions of architectural production has been the positing of the architectural object or element as a metaphor. To envision architecture, the dominant structuring metaphor in the Western philosophical tradition, as an embodiment of *trace,* or *archi-écriture,* or *différance* (words that cannot be defined [Derrida], but that are approached by metaphors of histos and weaving), is to remain well within the bounds of this tradition, as well as to miss the lesson that Derrida and Joyce offer. At a certain level of interpretation, Peter Eisenman's "present absences/absent presences" in the Carnegie Mellon Research Institute, however conceptually perverse in terms of the conventions of solid and void in architectural poché, remain solidly with the tradition of architecture as metaphor. The fact that what he terms *traces* are made material, trivializes (through metaphor, as metaphor will) Derrida's *trace.* The histological possibilities of architecture must lie both within the material construction that constitutes architecture itself ("always already" a weaving) and without it, as architecture bleeds out into spatio-temporality (beyond its material presence). And now, we have opened up the possibility of another reading of the Eisenman building. These material "traces," although they superficially obey the conventions of architectural symbolization of contemporaneous philosophical discourse, also, in their undecidability, can be read as markers (literal traces, not metaphors of traces) that serve as well-hidden (because they—lettres volées [LETTER]—are trivialized in plain sight) hints: places where secrets ooze from the box.[14] Now in other reading, we have a weaving of metaphor and metonymy, "an interlacing which permits the different threads and different lines of meaning—or of force—to go off again in different directions, just 'as it is always ready to tie itself up with others.'" (Derrida, *Margins*, 3).

VESSEL

"In the Nichtian glossery which purveys aprioric roots for aposteriorious tongues this is nat language at any sinse of the world and one might as fairly go and kish his sprogues as fail to certify whether the wartrophy eluded at some lives earlier was that somethink like a jug" (*FW*, 83.10–15).[15]

In Florida we are situated upon a most peculiar landscape. We stand upon a ground not of rock resting on rock but of the merest slice of solidity barely breaking the surface of the surrounding sea [POCHE]. Furthermore, the ground beneath our feet is not reliable, not the solid architecture of [STONE] piled on stone, carrying its loading in the proper compressive fashion, that we like our ground to be. It is in fact an architecture of holes and [CRYPT]s, filling and emptying with fluids, an architecture delineated by suction and secretion of solids, fluids, and gases, in such a complex and ever-changing configuration that to pin it down with a word seems illogical. But it *is* named by a word: Alachua, a word the previous residents of this place chose.[16] *Alachua:* Seminole for "a vessel or jug." Alachua, a land of filling and emptying, of holes and crypts, a place where the superimposition of "order" is ridiculous. A place where entire buildings are swallowed up, disappear into the surface of the ground, leaving behind only pock marks that will eventually fill with fluid. Consideration of such an architecture is not about imbuing a mundane thing with pumped-up significance, nor about projecting an image of the place. It is about how it works. Not concerned with what it means or what it looks like but what it does. The following construction is a [MAPPING] of this territory. It is the landscape of Poe—of the *Narrative of Arthur Gordon Pym,* for example—a territory of significant voids.

This construction consists of a collision of three texts: an essay by Martin Heidegger entitled "The Thing"; a character from Angela Carter's *Nights at the Circus,* Fanny Four-Eyes, who sports eyes on her breasts where nipples properly should be; and the text of architecture, which in its over-Booked and boxed-in state, is pocked with more booby traps than those of us who practice it would like to think [POCHE]. It is possible that there is a fourth text, an oscillating text, somewhat rudely forc'd.

In a happenstance that gives me more pleasure than I can say, this text intersects with the conclusion of Catherine Ingraham's review, entitled "Milking Deconstruction, or Cow Was the Show?" of the 1988 Deconstructivism show at the Museum of Modern Art. Here, Ingraham constructs a situation in which the contemporary architectural phenomenon of Deconstructivism is allegorized in the contemporary corporate agricultural phenomenon of the "necessity" to re-engineer the structure of the new, hormone-injected, super milk-giving cows in order to support their mammoth udders.

The idea of the cow as a thing—like the cow-thing [a jug] we fill with milk and set on our dinner table—is what makes the crude tampering with its bone structure possible. . . . Equally, the idea of deconstruction as a thing that can be built results in the crude surgeries of deconstructivism. It will ultimately be the shift in the idea of architectural structure—its dematerialization—that will interfere most substantially with the material surfaces of architecture, not so many jugs and pitchers cast in the shape of something called deconstructivism. (65)

Jugs and things are the objects of Heidegger's essay. If you will allow, I will recast this large and intricate vessel into a state that will accommodate an apprehension of a certain subtext. Despite the closure of space and time in the modern world, there is no nearness. We perceive that things are near to us, "but what is a thing?" "A jug is a thing. What is the jug? We say: a vessel, something of the kind that holds something else within it." "As a vessel the jug stands on its own as self-supporting." When we put it into our field of perception either through immediacy or representation, it becomes an object, yet it remains a vessel. The jug as a thing holds something. It is a container that must be made. When we understand it as a constructed vessel, we apprehend it as a thing, not as an object. We can never learn how the jug is by looking at its outward appearance; "the vessel's thingness does not lie at all in the material of which it consists, but in the void that holds." "Only a vessel . . . can empty itself." "How does the jug's void hold? It holds by taking what is poured in. It holds by keeping and retaining what it took in. The void holds in a twofold manner: taking and keeping. The word 'hold' is therefore ambiguous." "To pour from the jug is to give." "But the gift of the outpouring is what makes a jug a jug." Even the empty jug suggests the gift by a "non-admission" of which "a scythe . . . or a hammer is incapable." The thing is "nestling, malleable, pliant, compliant." The thing is "modestly compliant." "Inconspicuously compliant is the thing" ("The Thing," 166–182, *passim*).

Two Ways of Looking at a Jug

Aesthetic: "Stick 'em out just a little more. Yeah, now pull your tummy in all the way and let it out just a tad." Lifted and separated from the wall, the things appear twice their actual size and full and round as if to bursting. "Yeah, that's it. Now really push 'em up, hold your breath, keep your chin down. Give me the look, baby, give it to me, yeah, yeah. Great!" Click!

Scientific: "Now, you've got to get the whole thing up on the plate.

It'll feel a little cold, but it'll be over in a minute." The glass plate descends, pressing down, pressing, pressing the thing out to a horrifying, unrecognizable state: thin and flat, a broad, hideous slice of solidity criss-crossed with shocking blue lines. "Yes, that's it. Now hold your breath. Good!" Click!

" 'Well now that's done: and I'm glad it's over' " (Eliot, *Waste Land*, l. 252).

What is the secret that the firm, erect, sticking out thing holds? Unused, it is a frontier, where no man has gone before. What is the secret that lies beneath the power of this image, this object? What most desired and most feared thing is masked behind the desire to be the first, or the biggest? What does (M)other lack?

What is the secret that "oozes from the box?" Deleuze and Guattari suggest: "The secret must sneak, insert, or introduce itself into the arena of public forms; it must pressure them and prod known subjects into action.... Something must ooze from the box, something will be perceived through the box or in the half-opened box" (*Thousand Plateaus*, 287). Corporate architecture is a certain return of the repressed.

In Thomas Pynchon's novel *V.*, a novel whose entire 463 pages are devoted to the search for a figure who seems to be a woman, perhaps the mother of the protagonist, but who exists only in traces and hints, V. herself is masked by a seemingly infinite constellation of guises, forming the fetish construction that is the novel itself. Through the text there walks a figure known as the Bad Priest. Walks until, at a certain point of intersection, he falls down and falls apart, revealing himself to be a beautiful young woman who is in turn revealed, by the children and by the imagination of the narrator who dismantle her body, as a machinic assemblage of objects: glittering stones and precious metals, clocks, balloons, and lovely silks. The Bad Priest is a fetish construction mirroring the novel. As Alice Jardine has pointed out, it is "an assemblage of the dead objects that have helped hold together the narrative thus far" (*Gynesis*, 251). The Bad Priest and V. are reconstituted objects of desire, constructions of what is most desired and most feared. They are a rewriting of the urge to the aesthetic. (You will recall that aesthetics begins with the assemblage of the most beautiful, most perfect—and malleable, modestly compliant—woman by cutting the most desirable parts off many women and gathering them to make one woman-thing.) Like Pandora, whose box was not a box, but a jar, or jug. When the Bad Priest falls, the children cry, "It's a lady," and then: "She comes apart" (*V.*, 320–321). Into a "heap of broken images" (*Waste Land*, l. 22).

It's a Lady. Consider the Statue of Liberty, a fetish construction: she is a thing placed on a pedestal—to "lift and separate," to put on display. She is a spectacle. She is the hyper-reification of Luce Irigaray's gold-plated (in this case, copper-clad) woman: woman's body covered with commodities (make-up, fashion, capital, gold). "The cosmetics, the disguises of all kinds that women cover themselves with are intended to deceive, to promise more value than can be delivered. . . . Her body transformed into gold to satisfy his autoerotic, scopophiliac, and possessive instincts" (*Speculum*, 114).

This image of "Liberty for All" contains a secret, a purloined [LETTER] ingeniously hidden because it is there, in plain sight, a secret that calls into question the concepts of "Liberty" and "All." Beneath the surface of this woman's skin, beneath the implants that pump up the image, lies a "creeping disaster" [Irigaray], a crabby invasion, a crabgrass, a rhizome.

The Statue of Liberty is an allegory of desire and fear. It is a container, "a place where something is about to happen." [17] It is structure and envelope, image and machine. A gift. A Lady.

And she comes apart.

In the summer of 1987, a consortium of French institutions (including *L'Institut Français d'Architecture*) co-sponsored an international competition to design cultural artifacts commemorating the bicentenary of the French Revolution. The multidisciplinary and international intentions behind the competition were reinforced by the diversity of the jury, which ranged from philosopher Jean Baudrillard to structural engineer Peter Rice, and included writers, musicians, visual artists, and business people. The instructions for producing the commemorative artifacts were vague, leaving site, event commemorated, media, and dimensions to the discretion of the authors. Attracted by the indeterminacy, two friends (Durham Crout, a former student, and Robert Segrest) and I decided to participate.

Our project began as a project of exchange. As citizens of the United States constructing a monument to the French Revolution, we began with the simple idea of returning the gesture of the gift given by the French to commemorate the American Revolution. This gift, the Statue of Liberty, immediately generated a series of correspondences to other concepts delineated by the idea of gift: woman as presentation (both in the sense of the allegorical figure of Liberty and in the sense of woman as spectacle, as object of the gaze), woman as currency (both in the sense of the medium of exchange and in the sense of a flow that must be controlled, woman as fetish construction to be bestowed upon the imagination). We were struck by the way several constructs of power coincided in this woman-thing: war, aesthetics, the monumental, the reification of the female, history, the symbolic. We chose to commemorate an event of the French Revolution that bore potential correspondences to this construction of constructs, an event described by Marilyn French in *Beyond Power:* "When, on October 5 [1789], the market women discovered there was no bread in Paris, six thousand of them marched the twelve miles to Versailles to protest to the king personally. He promised to help them, and they marched triumphantly back to Paris with the royal family in tow" (191).

The itinerary that led to this choice is germane to understanding the project. Continuing along our line of the gift as generator, we selected nine sites on the body of the Statue of Liberty that are conventionally construed as (partial) objects of desire: eyes, lips, breasts, vulva, and so forth. These nine sites were made to correspond to nine sites of revolutionary points of intensity around the city of Paris through an operation involving sight lines, focal points, and the lens (a glassy instrument as well as the "mechanical" apparatus of the objectifying gaze). We then envisioned nine incisions upon the body of Liberty, slicing through each of the nine sites to produce nine generative sectional drawings [POCHE]. The irony of our operation resembling those of slasher films and pornography was not lost upon us. Our commentary through it upon the recent work of contemporary architects that is tethered to the "aura" of mutilated and murdered women we hope is not lost upon you. The nine sections were then to produce nine objects, to form a constellation of partial objects, which, in their assemblage, would form a certain "gift" to the French.

As is the way with well-laid plans, for a host of reasons including both fatigue and the powerful correspondence of the section through the eye and the site at the Palace at Versailles upon which it fell, we diverged from our original intention and chose to operate only upon the eye and the march of the six thousand market women on Versailles. The eye of the woman bears with it, after all, the potential to return the gaze; to return not merely in a sense of the conventional female acquiescence in sexual discourse, but also to re-turn, to deflect the power of the male gaze through a re-turn of the repressed, through the ex-orbitance of the female gaze. The project, then, reverses somewhat the mechanics of the *fascinus,* a phallus-shaped amulet for warding off the "evil eye" of the fascinating woman [ROCKET]. The evil eye, and to whom it belongs, is called into question.

The *unseen* in the body is critical here. Sectioning the statue is an act of incision and release. The incision marks the temporal and geographical point at which the image of the body gives way to the possibilities of the body. It becomes a gift of another kind, an insidious gift, with unseen agents hiding within, like the Trojan Horse. This hollow vessel, this monument, this gift to the state, holds within it the potential of undermining the state. In the Trojan Horse, the body masks the body politic. The Trojan Horse is a viral architecture: a sleek protein coat with invasive content [MINOR ARCHITECTURE].

The incision marking the initiation of generation is repeated as an incising inscription. A slash three hundred meters long and a meter square in section is made in the forecourt of the Palace. This repetition is simultaneously a reflection ([MIRROR]: an other kind of repetition) of an already-there gash in the earth on the other side of the Palace: the Grand Canal, a commanding axis of inscription terminating in a statue. Thus, what marks the termination of the grand axis is the same (vessel, statue) as what marks the initiation of our project. And again, this identity is marked in reverse, setting the project into interminable reflexivity: the western end of the trench stops abruptly at the base of another statue: that of Louis Quatorze atop a (perhaps now suspicious) horse. The new incision (the trench) reflects the old (the Grand Canal); the radical project mimics the state project. Furthermore, it is a rational response to the existing topography: our trench is a physically inscribed reflection of the relation of the incision of the Grand Canal with the vertical slicing plane of the west (mirrored) wall of the Hall of Mirrors. In other words, we have taken the image of what one would see if one could see through the mirror and projected it back into the world before the mirror, reversing the customary relation of "reality" and "image" in the mirror. In this "geography of the imagination," the idea that the mirror is utterly contained within its grandiose vessel—the Palace—appears simultaneously negligible and crucial.

The reflection works at another level as well. If one renders malleable the word for our gift, *un cadeau*, into a Franco-Italian hybrid of *ca'* *d'eau*, there is here a [HOUSE] of water (a body), which parodies the wateriness, the flow, of the Grand Canal. A *ca' d'eau* is a house of currency. The trench functions as a monumental *pissoir*, open to the public in a public place. But being pissed off, here, is a redundant gesture. Nestled (modestly and compliantly) in the floor of the trench are six thousand vessels, with pearlike shapes and copper skins. Each is lined with mirror tain and glass and each is full of body fluids. Their bodily secrets allow them to laugh away or write off the oppression of being pissed on. These reproducing cells (vessels, fluid-filled uteri) mirror a something disastrous going on beneath the surface of the court of history, of power. It is the injection into a Revolution of "Feed Our Children." An injection of what is more "powerful than" (beyond) power. A giving suck, an other—although not the other—side of a suck taken. A gift.

Its borders incised with alchemical glyphs signifying moons and months and body fluids [HIEROGLYPH] and marked by crisscrossing sutures of iron rods, this trench, this slice of void [POCHE] barely breaking the surface tension of its surrounds, gives up its secret—a secret marked, as things that must remain properly hidden often are, with an X. The X is an emblem of Heidegger's fourfold, in which "each of the four mirrors in its own way the presence of the others" ("The Thing," 179). X is a generic substitute for a thing. The thing is "nestling, malleable, pliant, compliant, nimble." Heidegger suggests circularity (O), but there is an X hidden here, an unknown, a secret. Heidegger's thing folds the fourfold along a hinge, which he suggests is a mirroring. Remember that an X hinged is two V's folded at the point of intersection, the place where the secret is both enfolded and released. X is the doubled perspective on two canals intersecting in a mirror. It is a vanishing point. To X is "to cancel or obliterate with or as if with a series of x's." "Cross your heart"—and hope to die and stick your finger in your eye. X is a cartoon convention marking "lidless eyes" (*Waste Land*, l. 138) blinded by a surprise or blow to the head. As Catherine Ingraham has pointed out, the crisscross of heavy mascara marks "eyes which do not see"—eyes that do not look beyond the look. X is a mark of nonidentity, a nonidentifying signature, like that of a person who is identified by the name of her father that, in a mirroring, is replaced by the name of her husband. Yet X is a chiasmus, signifying the alchemical androgyne—"blind, throbbing between two lives."[18] X is a kiss, both a patronizing and a nurturing gesture. A puckering, a sucking, an undulating architecture of solids, liquids, and gases.

A reverse fascinus, warding off the evil eye represented by the eye of the "one-eyed trouser snake" of Joyce, the Cyclopean eye of power invested in the Palace, the project is a defetishizing move, inviting the (male) body, refusing the power structure of the phallus that represses and corrupts the male body, and displaying the profound return of the repressed of the female body through an obscuring, a darkening, of the image, and a display of the generative—the jug is not a thing, but a magical machine—an interwoven system of apparatuses, a text.

"And Schreck would say: 'Look at him, Fanny.' So Fanny would take off her blindfold and give him a beaming smile.

"Then Madame Schreck would say: 'I said, *look* at him, Fanny.' At which she'd pull up her shift.

"For, where she should have had nipples, she had eyes.

"Then Madame Schreck would say: 'Look at him properly, Fanny.' Then those two other eyes of hers would open.

"They were a shepherd's blue, same as the eyes in her head; not big, but very bright.

"I asked her once, what did she see with those mammillary eyes, and she says: 'Why, same as with the top ones but lower down.'" (Carter, *Nights at the Circus,* 69)

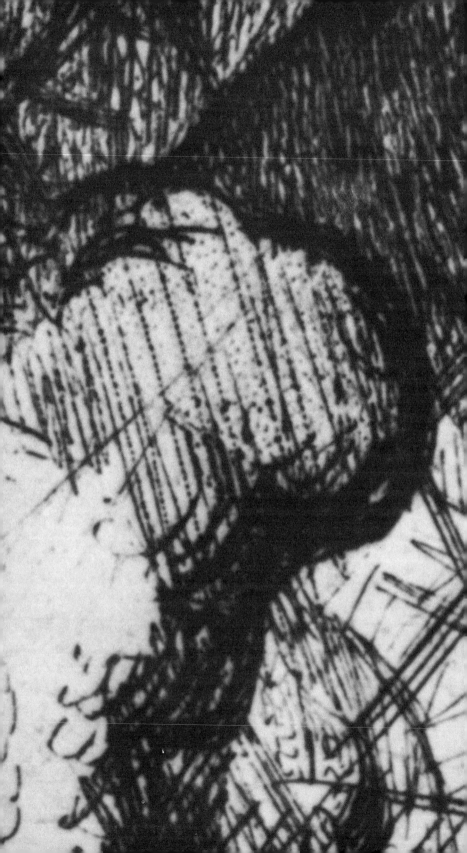

Notes

A Priming

The notation following citations to *Finnegans Wake* throughout the book reflects the convention in Joyce scholarship of citing both the page/s and the line/s of text referred to in the *Wake*. All references within the text are to the Penguin edition, 1939; © 1967 by George and Lucia Joyce. Used by permission of Viking Penguin.

1. For a succinct introduction to these critical strategies, see Vincent Leitch, *Deconstructive Criticism*.

2. This list could be extended infinitely. The particular pairs listed here appear because they delineate particular binary territory mapped by this construction.

3. One of the "untrustworthy bridges" that Derrida takes to task is metaphor, a problematic of conventional writing of which I am painfully aware. The metaphorical aspect of this "map" (this book) is only a part of its constitution—i.e., it is not *essentially* metaphorical.

4. An analogous connection might be made between the pair *construction* and *architecture*, enveloping both a "narrow" sense of *construction* and another sense that is revelatory of certain repressions. This connection will figure prominently in this text.

5. The *Ursprung* was written from 1924 to 1925 and published in 1928. By 1931, it was, as George Steiner points out in the introduction to the 1977 English translation, "literally . . . extinct" (7), because of the Nazi purge of writings by German Jews. A few copies survived in the hands of friends and in the precious libraries of refugees. *Finnegans Wake* was written between 1922 and 1939, published in 1939. Joyce, a consummate consumer of contemporary European culture and a denizen of cafes and coffee houses in France, Italy, and Switzerland, may well have known of the *Ursprung* and its structure, even if he had not read the text itself.

6. The root meaning of *glyph* is "to carve," and *write* comes from an Old English word meaning "to tear" or "scratch."

7. We might usefully swerve at this point to Manfredo Tafuri's connection of Piranesi and Sergei Eisenstein, the "master of montage," in "Dialectics of the Avant-garde," an article that is followed by a translation of Eisenstein's essay, "Piranesi, or the Fluidity of Forms."

8. A model that, as Marco Frascari has reminded me, Ferdinand de Saussure (*Course in General Linguistics*) used to describe the syntagmatic structure of language.

9. A trajectory to Walter Benjamin's "Work of Art in the Age of Mechanical Reproduction" (in *Illuminations*), with its powerful thesis on art and politics, would lend support to this statement.

10. These questions are appropriated from Deleuze and Guattari, who write in *Anti-Oedipus,* "The unconscious poses no problem of meaning, solely problems of use. The question posed by desire is not 'What does it mean?' but rather *'How does it work?'*. . . Desire makes its entry with the general collapse of the question 'What does it mean?' " (109)

11. This story is a dominant thematic of this construction. The connection between the letter of Poe's story and that of Joyce's text is highly significant.

12. By this I mean that the apprehension (interpretation, deconstruction of the language, units of construction) of *Finnegans Wake* depends upon a simultaneous grasp of both the master language in which it appears to have been written and the involutions and convolutions gesturing toward, approaching, or even reaching other "languages" that pock its syntactical-semantic territory. This is the linguistic side. On the architectural, or rather, architectonic, side, the same concept is operating: the structures, the geometries, etc., are always sliding into others, so that more than one structural system is always perceptible, and they are never really separable. Borromini's San Carlino or Soane's 12–13 Lincoln's Inn Fields may serve as analogues (albeit tentative, simple ones, despite their relative architectural complexities) to this architectonic.

13. *Grasped* is a crucial word. The Greek word *syllapsies* means "grasping" and refers to assemblages. It also had at one time the connotation of "conception" or "pregnancy." Grasping the simultaneity suggests a collapse of space and time, and offers a key to the reading of this work (as well as that of Joyce).

14. The differences and relations of architectural history and the history of architecture have been explored at length by Marco Frascari.

Chapter I: Allegory and the Possibility of Architecture

This chapter was written in the summer of 1988 in a room overlooking a cow pasture near Cambridge, England. It was presented in September of 1988 at a working session on Architectural Theory held at the Chicago Institute of Architecture and Urbanism. It appears as "A lay a stone a patch a post a pen the ruddyrun: Minor Architectural Possibilities" in the documentation of that session, *Strategies of Architectural Thinking,* ed. John Whiteman, Jeffrey Kipnis, and Richard Burdett

(Cambridge, Mass.: MIT Press, 1992). Reprinted by permission of MIT Press. Citations from Walter Benjamin *Origin of German Tragic Drama,* are to the edition translated by John Osborne (London: Verso/NLB, 1977), © 1977 Verso/NLB. Used by permission of Verso.

1. The reader has just encountered the first indication that this project is a historical one. See Manfredo Tafuri, "The Historical Project," in *Sphere and Labyrinth.*

2. I refer to the exhibition "Deconstructivist Architecture," mounted by the Museum of Modern Art in 1988. It was curated by Philip Johnson and Mark Wigley, and it included the work of Peter Eisenman, Frank Gehry, Zaha Hadid, Coop Himmelblau, Rem Koolhaas, Daniel Libeskind, and Bernard Tschumi.

3. A mystorical element: growing up in East Tennessee, I recited the Pledge of Allegiance in Latin every school day of my adolescent life.

4. The following paragraphs represent an oblique commentary upon Robert Segrest's "Frank Lloyd Wright at the Midway," in Whiteman, Kipnis, and Burdett, *Strategies of Architectural Thinking.*

5. The prison house here refers both to the type (that which Piranesi exploded in *Le Carceri*) and to the metaphor of language indicated in Fredric Jameson's *Prison-House of Language.* Mark Taylor connects these prisons and others in "Deadlines: Approaching Anarchetecture," in *Tears.*

6. It is interesting to note that the *-ballein,* "to throw," of *emballein* is also the etymological root of the *-bol* of *symbol,* "to throw together."

7. *Symballein* is the antonym of *diaballein,* "to throw across," from which *devil* and *diabolic* come. The allegorical posited here contains aspects of the symbolic and the diabolic.

8. Michel Foucault: "[Heterotopias are] the disorder in which fragments of a large number of possible orders glitter separately. . . . Heterotopias are disturbing, probably because they secretly undermine language, because they make it impossible to name this and that, because they destroy 'syntax' in advance, and not only the syntax with which we construct sentences but also that less apparent syntax which causes words and things (next to and also opposite to one another) to 'hold together' " (*Order of Things* xviii).

9. I build here upon Derrida's pun on "The Purloined Letter" in *The Post Card,* p. 423. Derrida takes Poe's story for his subject because it was the subject of Jacques Lacan's "Seminar." The fact that "The Purloined Letter" was translated into the French story *"La Lettre volée"* by Charles Baudelaire, the poet of spleen (melancholy) and flowers of evil, and the subject of Walter Benjamin's analysis, may or may not be important here.

10. The itinerary through Craig Owens ("The Allegorical Impulse") to Robert Smithson ("A Sedimentation of Mind: Earth Projects") to Edgar Allan Poe (*The Narrative of Arthur Gordon Pym*) and, one might add, to the holey space of

Gilles Deleuze and Félix Guattari in *Mille Plateaux* [*A Thousand Plateaus*], maps a kind of underground passage to many others here.

11. Jameson's blind spots (construing the "third world" as an entity and the "first world" as white, heterosexual male) have been well-illuminated by Aijaz Ahmad in "Jameson's Rhetoric of Otherness," so I will not dwell on them here.

12. This bit of mapping tracks a conduit via Heraclitus' Fragment LXXX ("The hidden attunement is better than the obvious one"), here marking a paradoxical chiasmus at the site of the purloined letter to chapter 2 of this book. (All quotations from Heraclitus are translated by Charles Kahn and found in *The Art and Thought of Heraclitus*.)

13. It should be abundantly clear, on the evidence of the gender of the producers (Piranesi and Joyce) of the works in question, that my use of "the feminine" does not have a simple connection to gender. However, it is my belief that the propensity (the pent-up rage, pent-up desires) to "write the feminine" exists perhaps closer to release in those human beings whose existences have been dominated by forms of oppression, i.e., those who benefit least from the status quo. Women, persons of color, lesbians and gay men, the poor, and nomadic people (including the "homeless") fall into this category. Indeed, the majority of human beings on this planet fall into this category, pointing to the subtlety and power of phallogocentric culture, the culture of Catch-22. Catch-22 is a wall or cage. Writing the feminine is mole work, writing on the wall.

14. A voyeur without eyes is ex-orbitant.

15. See Hélène Cixous, "Writing as Poison or Cure," in *Exile of Joyce*, 741–745.

16. An additional error here, interesting because of the chains of textual relations it generates, is Jameson's misnaming of the Westin Bonaventure, which he repeatedly calls the Bonaventura. Many have jumped to correct Jameson's error, including N. Katherine Hayles, who gets it wrong by reversing the names, in *Chaos Bound*, and Edward W. Soja, who corrects more persuasively in *Postmodern Geographies*.

17. As this book goes to publication, Sarah is twelve and wants to be a veterinarian, "small animals only."

18. Mark Taylor: "As the irreducible interval in which time and space interweave, *différance* is the *'matrix'* of all presence and absence" (*Altarity*, 276).

19. A statement that has been in some ways strengthened and in some ways challenged by the erasure of the wall, an event that was virtually unthinkable when I began this book.

I would like to address the difficult problematic of the presence of Peter Eisenman in this work. Eisenman's production over the past two decades has in large part constituted the nourishment that has sustained the growth of my thinking about architecture. And certainly not only mine: I have many siblings. Perhaps my brothers have killed Pater to their satisfaction and no longer suffer angstuous influenzas.

The problem of the daughter may be different. For me, it is a problem of locating the excluded middle: not to kill Dad but not to live invisibly in his shadow. It is perhaps a task of living tangibly in the shadow, making of the shadow something else that is my own, that abandons the linearity of comparison and embraces its own otherness. While Peter Eisenman is much named here, the construction itself contains an implicit critique of his work, a critique that recognizes a reflexivity among its objects and its genealogy (which includes Tafuri and Benjamin, as well). My project is neither to revere nor to murder, but to recognize the perhaps more complex entanglement of the father-daughter relationship. Wrestling and copulation have their similarities, after all. (I learned this from my [m]other father, James Joyce.)

But perhaps it all boils down to a statement from that great distiller, Jeffrey Kipnis. Visiting his apartment in New York, I pulled a fountain pen out of my bag to jot something down. Jeff noted in that way of his, both deadpan and filled with sophomoric significance, "You know, you and Peter have the same pen."

Chapter 2: Three Constructions

This construction was assembled in the spring of 1984 on the floors and walls of an old, beautiful, leaking apartment in midtown Atlanta. It was made as a term paper for a philosophy course taught by Angel Medina, whose support and encouragement were pure nourishment during the difficult time of the breakup of my first marriage and the general animosity toward my work from my professors. It appeared in an earlier form as "'La région où s'érige le désir sans contrainte': Piranesi's *Campo Marzio* Misread," in *Art Papers* in the summer of 1984.

The discovery years later of Rachel Blau DuPlessis' resonant but much more substantial collaborative construction, "For the Etruscans" (see *The Pink Guitar*) was very satisfying to me. Her/their collage-essay shows more explicitly what I was after here. As a marker of an important detour, I have added the opening quotation.

1. This collection of semi-attributed borrowings mirrors Piranesi's own strategy in the *Campo Marzio,* which is a collage of half-recognizable images drawn from life, earlier sources, and Piranesi's own imagination. None of the borrowings should be identified too exactly.

2. This lovely term refers to Guy Davenport's collection of essays, *The Geography of the Imagination.*

3. This is, of course, a description of the origin of the "Trojan game," the city-founding ritual of marking a labyrinth in the earth.

4. At this point lies a trajectory and an indebtedness to the work of Ann Bergren, who has woven the worlds of classics, architecture, and women together into stunning, glittering mantles. For more about Metis and Penelope, see her "Architecture Gender Philosophy," in *Strategies of Architectural Thinking,* ed. Whiteman, Kipnis, and Burdett, and "Mouseion."

5. The "lace apron," which refers to the anatomy of adipose tissue, a slippery yellow web of strands of various thicknesses, is a generative emblem here. It appears again explicitly and implicitly throughout this construction.

6. The multivalency of the feminine river as passage and its relation to the ambiguity in the title of Benjamin's *Passagen-Werk* will not go unnoted.

7. This section was constructed in the summer and fall of 1985. It originated as a map of its V-points scrawled on the ell of two blackboard walls in an unused summer classroom. With things drawn and stuck on and with a lace apron of strings and lines running everywhere. It appeared in an earlier form as "Vertex and Vortex: A Tectonics of Section," in *Perspecta,* and later, in altered form, in *Drawing/Building/ Text,* edited by Andrea Kahn. It takes on yet another aspect here.

8. This is part of a mnemonic device for the listing in order of their occurrence the cranial nerves. *Viewed* is the mnemonic for the *vagus* nerve.

9. I cannot resist pointing out that there is at play here an unbearable lightness of received truth. I am fascinated by the absence of the obvious, that is, the gender of those who have revealed what women want.

10. *C HOPKINS CaFe, Mighty good, Naturally Clean* is a mnemonic device for the constituents of protoplasm: Carbon, Hydrogen, Oxygen, Phosphorus, Potassium (K), Iodine, Nitrogen, Sulfur, Calcium, Iron (Fe), Magnesium, Sodium (Na), and Chlorine.

11. *Stencil* is Herbert Stencil, the protagonist of *V.,* whose name translated into French is *Pochoir.*

12. *Webster's Third New International Dictionary* defines *deferent* thus: "n. 1: an imaginary circle surrounding the earth in whose periphery, acc. to Ptolemy, either the celestial body or the center of its epicycle is supposed to move   adj. 2: serving to carry out or down; deferential."

13. Compare this to Joyce's "painful digests," part of the contents of the House O'Shea/House O'Shame.

14. The preceding paragraphs are taken from "Interval," the text of a talk I gave at Yale, published in *Art Papers,* July/August, 1985.

15. Charles Kahn points out that the initial word (*syllapsies*) has by others been translated "connections" and "assemblages," and that for Aristotle the word could have meant "conception" or "pregnancy" (see *Art and Thought of Heraclitus*).

16. *La taupe* is an underminer introduced by Hélène Cixous and Catherine Clément in *The Newly Born Woman* (*La jeune née*).

17. Betsy Wing, the translator of *The Newly Born Woman* (*La Jeune née*), points out that the phrase "En voila du propre!" (the English equivalent of which is "What a fine mess!") is used in the text in places where what is "appropriate" is called into question.

18. "Dark-brained" should remind the reader of the title of Marguerite Yourcenar's essay "The Dark Brain of Piranesi," in *The Dark Brain of Piranesi and Other Essays.*

19. The tarantella, a dance whose origins lie in the manic movements of individuals purportedly bitten by spiders, is an important motif in *The Newly Born Woman.* Clément writes, "In a region of the Mezzogiorno in southern Italy, where the

colonies of Magna Graecia were once established, there are women said to have been bitten by tarantulas. These spider bites—these tarantula bites—that cause depression, convulsions, dizziness, and migraines have made them ill. But because tarantulas do not exist in this region, we have to conclude that these are psychical phenomena" (19). She then cites several passages from Ernesto di Martino, who demonstrated the connection between the tarantella and hysteria. (In *La Terre du Remords* and *Sertum de papale de venenis*.) In one passage, di Martino describes "a crisis . . . especially before marriage . . . set loose by eros in several forbidden ways" (*Terre*). Clément continues: "During the crisis, they become spider, cow, lizard, goat" (21).

20. The phrase "psychical house" is from Cixous and Clément, *Newly Born Woman*, p. 12.

A decoding of Joyce's passage is appropriate here. A cataleptic (a state of paralysis in which body parts remain wherever they are placed) or catalytic (material used in a chemical reaction to increase its rate, the material itself remaining unchanged by the reaction) misce-phallic/mis-cephalic/myth of phallic (plus Mithraic—ancient male mystery cult—and Mithridates—king of ancient times who regularly ingested small quantities of poison, thereby gaining immunity to it [a pharmakon]). Was this *Totem Fulcrum Est* (the family emblem is the bed/post/phallus, the totem is—after all—a pole) Ancestor yu hald in *Dies Eirae* you halled/hailed/held in this area/day of ire/day of Ireland/desire) where no spider webbeth (a proper, clean—*propre*—place).

21. It should be abundantly apparent that the primary father in question here is Manfredo Tafuri, the coiner of the phrase, "delirious constructions" (*Sphere and the Labyrinth*, 11). The English equivalent of "fare il passo piu lungo della gamba," is "to bite off more than one can chew." "Avere la tarantola," "to have the tarantula," is the same as "to have ants in one's pants."

22. *Joyceful* has been coined by many, but for me most meaningfully by my daughter Sarah, who, at age four and living with a newly single mother in the early stages of this book, declared her preference for one room of our new apartment over another because, "Mom, it's just more joyceful."

23. This construction was written in the winter of 1987 and was first given as a keynote address for the symposium, "Type and the (Im)possibilities of Convention," held at the University of Minnesota in May 1987. It was published, in slightly altered form, as "Tip Tap Type Tope," in *Midgård 2, Type and the (Im)possibilities of Convention*. And it appears here in a third incarnation.

24. The conference took place in September 1985. Although Professors Ellmann and Derrida were most kind to me, I can still feel the hairs on the back of my neck perk up whenever this evening comes to mind. To make matters worse, Gayatri Spivak—my heroine—was in the audience. I ached for her approval; I did not get it.

25. Importantly in "Lestrygonians," Joyce suggests how the body (the hungry stomach, the aching loins) secretly influences rationality. Desire can invade and undermine rational thinking.

26. In the spirit of Vico and Joyce, I have constructed here a creative ety-

mology. The traditional Indo-European roots of *architect* are *arkhein*, "to rule," from which comes *arch-*, as in archangel or arch-villain, and *teks*, "to weave." I have made *arch-* into the more benign and architectural *arch*, whose Indo-European root is *arkw*, "bow and arrow." Thus, my architect is less a master builder and more an individual who weaves constructions with arches—curves, swerves, and tangents.

27. The connection between the compass joint and the pelvic joints of those *daidalons* that walked was offered me by Marco Frascari, while chiding me for my "vague" use (in another paper) of *vague*, a word that comes from the Latin verb *vago*, "I walk or wander." *Vago* is also the progenetrix of *vagary* and the vagus nerve of construction 2. The movement of the compass out of its proper place in architectural instrumentation (its definition as an instrument of dissemination in addition to its being an instrument of emplotment) should come as no surprise: it simply got up and walked.

28. Joyce's phrase was "the lingerous longerous book of the dark" (*FW*, 251.24), referring to his own book as well as to the Egyptian Book of the Dead. But the phrase also points to the title of John Bishop's *Joyce's Book of the Dark*.

29. I appropriate this question from its obvious source in popular culture but more immediately, with all connections intentional, from Robert Segrest, "The Perimeter Projects."

30. This particular etching is a part of the *Opere varie di Architettura,* published in 1743, and therefore is contemporary with, but not part of, the *Invenzioni Caprice di Carceri.* The latter work, consisting of fourteen plates and known as the first state *Carceri,* or Prisons, was thought to have been published in 1745, although Piranesi later noted that the plates were produced in 1742. The so-called second state *Carceri,* or *Carceri d'invenzione di G. B. Piranesi,* consisting of sixteen plates, was published in 1761.

31. During the years of its composition (1922–1939), *Finnegans Wake* was known as *Work in Progress.*

32. *Dor* is both a passage or hatch and a gift (from its Greek root). *Finnegans Wake* itself is a gift "of ambiguous purpose," a Trojan horse (like Pasiphaë's cow, a vessel), a gift horse to be looked in the mouth, or door.

Chapter 3: Construction Three-Plus-One

This chapter was written in a shorter version in the spring of 1987, for presentation at the International Association for Philosophy and Literature Conference on "Postmodernism," Lawrence, Kansas, May 1987. The paper was first published as "In the Museyroom" in *Assemblage 5*, ed. K. Michael Hays, © 1987 by MIT Press, and later in *Philosophical Streets*, ed. Dennis Crow (Moulins les Metz: Maisonneuve Press, 1990).

1. The etchings were published in *Différentes vues de quelques restes de trois grands edifices qui subsistent encore dans le milieu de l'ancienne ville de Pesto,* 1778.

2. The river Liffey flows through the landscape of *Finnegans Wake* in many guises, most frequently as Anna Livia Plurabelle (ALP: *Anna* is Gaelic for "river," *Livia* is the Latin version of "Liffey," and *Plurabelle* is Latin for "of many beauties"), and is usually coded by "LIF" or "LIV" in the text. The numbers eleven and thirty-two—respectively the "begin again" number after one has used up all one's fingers in counting and the number of feet per second per second at which a falling object falls—recur constantly throughout Joyce's text, as here in "Thirty-two West Eleventh streak," the address of HCE and ALP, which is named in lines *12* and *13* on page 274.

3. See Sir John Summerson, *A New Description of Sir John Soane's Museum.*

4. The "*Bug of the Deaf*," besides being an allusion to one of the major conceptual structures of the *Wake* (the Egyptian Book of the Dead), is, of course, also an earwig, or (H. C.) earwicker. "*How to Pull a Good Horuscoup even when Oldsire is Dead to the World*" (105.28–29), one of the dozens of alternative titles to *Finnegans Wake* listed on pages 104–107, invokes both Horus and Osiris, thus making another of the numerous allusions to the Book of the Dead, demonstrating its importance to Joyce. It seems worth noting here that the Book of the Dead, a book always rewritten for each "owner," was a kind of guidebook.

5. Here, I have "bilked the best." The Jacks are lifted from Guy Davenport, "The House That Jack Built," in *Geography of the Imagination*: "*Finnegans Wake* is the house Jack Joyce built, but is is a reading of the Old Testament, the house that Jacob built, and of the New Testament, the house that the carpenter Jack Christ built. It is a world of involuted meaning like the house that Jack Ruskin built, Ruskin being the Shaun to Charles Dodgson's Shem" (49).

6. In editing this book, Susan Laity asked about the meaning of the "unauthorized quotation," which has gone unnoted in previously published versions of this essay. "A feminist architecture is not architecture at all," is an assertion I made in a panel discussion once, when asked what a feminist architecture would be. (I believe I followed it with, "The phrase 'feminist architecture' is an oxymoron.") Several months later, this assertion appeared in an article by Robert Segrest ("Frank Lloyd Wright at the Midway"), without quotation marks and without citation. And so, I have here stolen back from my husband my own words, which formed an unauthorized quotation when he used them, and are perhaps now doubly unauthorized. Perhaps the community property laws protect us both from what sharp-eyed Susan perceived as potential legal trouble.

7. See Jacques Derrida, "Two Words for Joyce," in Attridge and Ferrer, *Post-Structuralist Joyce.*

Chapter 3 + 1: Syllapsies
1. This is a fragment of the first of the hundred-letter "thunder words" disseminated throughout *Finnegans Wake*. These words serve as signals (cf. the Heraclitean fragment "The thunder bolt pilots all things"). Although they appear to be

glossolalic, they are in fact well-loaded portmanteaus, packed with bits of words referring to thunder in dozens of languages.

2. All elisions but the first in this particular text, bracketed and not, are Derrida's.

3. This translation was begun by me and completed with the help of Professor Paolo Valesio of Yale. My thanks to him.

4. I refer to the Abbaye Laugier's 1753 tale of the "savage," who, finding the darkness and foul air of the cave intolerable, constructs a dwelling from tree branches that "does not bury him": four branch posts, four branch beams, and a roof of gabled branches. "All the splendors of architecture ever conceived have been modeled on the little rustic hut I have just described" (*Essay on Architecture*, 11–12).

5. I refer to the end of "The Work of Art in the Age of Mechanical Reproduction" in *Illuminations*.

6. This phrase has been appropriated from the title of an unpublished collection of poems, "Pigeon Coup," by David Fraley, an architect in Atlanta who paints houses and canvases and weaves words.

7. The translation of this line comes from Cixous, *Exile of James Joyce*, p. 744. Cixous quotes the note as it appeared in "La Pharmacie de Platon," and Purcell's translation allows for the ambiguity upon which I rely (and upon which, though of course not by virtue of the translation, Cixous relies as well). This ambiguity lies in the word *cet*, which means both "this" and "that." By translating it "this" (as does Purcell) rather than "that" (as does Barbara Johnson in her English translation of *Dissemination*), the demonstrative pronoun's referent oscillates between "Bataille's text" (which appears in the same sentence before the semicolon) and Derrida's text: "The paragraph that is about to end here will have marked the fact that this pharmacy of Plato's also brings into play [*entraine*] Bataille's text, inscribing within the story of the egg the sun of the accursed part [*la part maudite*]; the whole of [this/that] essay, as will quickly become apparent, being itself nothing but a reading of *Finnegans Wake*." This translation is Johnson's, with my insertion of the "this/that" switching mechanism.

8. Robinson refers to Audre Lorde's essay "The Master's Tools Will Never Dismantle the Master's House," in Moraga and Anzaldúa, *This Bridge Called My Back*. The architectural metaphors at work here—house and bridge—should not go unnoted.

9. I refer to the network of essays generated from Jacques Lacan's "Seminar on 'The Purloined Letter.'" These include Jacques Derrida, "Le Facteur [factor, postman] de la verité," in *La Carte Postale* and also (in slightly different form) in "The Purveyor of Truth"; Barbara Johnson, "The Frame of Reference"; and Jane Gallop, "The American Other," in *Reading Lacan*.

10. One of my husband's and my all-time greatest quarrels occurred as we tromped around the Castello Sant'Angelo in the broiling Roman summer heat. I don't recall what the quarrel was about (its meaning); only its effect.

11. These are fragments from a letter from Guy Davenport, upon whom I

have never laid eyes, but with whom I have enjoyed a correspondence over the period of production of this book. And to whom, as I have come to realize now that this work is almost over, I am indebted more than was ever in my consciousness. The letter is printed here with his permission.

12. This reproduces the text of one of several postcards sent to Peter Eisenman over the summer of 1988. The idea was that I would write and send them, he would collect them with their ghosty postmarks, give them back to me, and I would weave them as graphics into an essay I was to write for the Ohio State Eisenman monograph. I have not written the essay and Peter has not returned the cards, but every time I see him he mentions that he still has them (these little letters of mine, now a double lack, another chateau des cartes).

13. Having grown up among countryfolk in East Tennessee and Southwest Virginia, where conditions of scarcity spawned invention as a way of living, I find bell hooks's proposal that black slave women were the first to make crazy quilts, and for themselves, not as objects d'art for the wives of slave-owners, thoroughly persuasive. Her essay on quilts, "Aesthetic Inheritances: history worked by hand," is a strong construction of "fragments, bits and pieces of information found here and there," inspired by her grandmother, Sarah Hooks Oldham ("Baba"). See her *Yearning,* pages 115–122.

14. When Eisenman lectures on this project, he calls these "present absences" "bananas," in reference to their forms. But also: " '[The contractors] were going bananas over the cubes,' Mr. Eisenman says. 'They were really getting off on it' " (Taylor, "Mr. In-Between," 52).

15. This section, originally entitled "Jugs," was written for a symposium, "Body/Space/Machine," held at the University of Florida in March 1989. In expanded form, but one different from the way it appears here, "Jugs" was first published as "Big Jugs" in *The Hysterical Male: new feminist theory,* ed. Marilouise and Arthur Kroker.

16. Our house in Florida was located a stone's throw from one of the numerous sinkholes in Alachua County, Florida. The architecture building at the University of Florida, where I worked, is located at the edge of another.

17. These are the words of Aldo Rossi, whose obsession with the idea of architecture as vessel is well-known and well-documented. See *A Scientific Autobiography.*

18. The androgyne here is Tiresias, in Eliot's *Waste Land* (cf. l. 218), blinded because his androgynous experience led him to speak the unspeakable (that the female's pleasure—*jouissance*—in sex is greater than that of the male).

Bibliography

Adcock, Craig E. *Marcel Duchamp's Notes from the* Large Glass: *An N-Dimensional Analysis*. Ann Arbor: UMI Research Press, 1983.

Ahmad, Aijaz. "Jameson's Rhetoric of Otherness and the 'National Allegory.'" *Social Text* 17 (1897): 3–25.

Atherton, J. S. *The Books at the* Wake. New York: Viking Press, 1960.

Attridge, Derek, and Daniel Ferrer, eds. *Post-Structuralist Joyce*. Cambridge: Cambridge University Press, 1984.

Barthes, Roland. *Critical Essays*. Translated by Richard Howard. Evanston, Ill.: Northwestern University Press, 1972.

——. *Empire of Signs* (1970). Translated by Richard Howard. New York: Hill and Wang, 1982.

Bataille, Georges. *Visions of Excess (Selected Writings, 1927–1939)*. Edited by Allan Stoekl; translated by Allan Stoekl, with Carl R. Lovitt and Donald M. Leslie, Jr. Minneapolis: University of Minnesota Press, 1985.

Beckett, Samuel. "Dante . . . Bruno. Vico . . . Joyce." In *Our Exagmination Round His Factification For Incamination of Work in Progress*. Paris: Shakespeare and Company, 1929.

Benjamin, Walter. *Illuminations* (1955). Edited by Hannah Arendt; translated by Harry Zohn. New York: Schocken Books, 1969.

——. "N [Theoretics of Knowledge; Theory of Progress (from *Passagen-Werk*)]," *The Philosophical Forum* 15, 1–2 (Fall-Winter 1983–84): 1–40.

——. *The Origin of German Tragic Drama*. (*Ursprung des deutschen Trauerspiels*, 1928). Translated by John Osborne. London: New Left Books, 1985.

Bergren, Ann L. T. "Language and the Female in Early Greek Thought." *Arethusa* 16, 1–2 (1983): 69–95.

——. "Mouseion: Muse I am. Memory and the Fetish in the Buildings and Murals of Venice, CA." In *Fetish*, edited by Sarah Whiting and Greg Lynn, 130–157. Princeton, N.J.: Princeton Architectural Press, 1992.

Bishop, John. *Joyce's Book of the Dark:* Finnegans Wake. Madison: University of Wisconsin Press, 1986.

Bloomer, Jennifer. "Interval." *Art Papers,* 9, 4 (1985): 6–11.

——. "In the Museyroom." *Assemblage 5* (1987): 58–65.

——. " 'La Région où s'érige le désir sans contrainte': Piranesi's *Campo Marzio* Misread." *Art Papers 5* (1984): 37–44.

——. "Tip Tap Type Tope." *Midgård 2* (1992): 33–45.

——. "Toward Desiring Architecture." In *Drawing/Building/Text,* edited by Andrea Kahn. Princeton, N.J.: Princeton Architectural Press, 1991.

——. "Vertex and Vortex: A Tectonics of Section." *Perspecta* (The Yale Architectural Journal) 23 (1987): 38–53.

Borges, Jorgé Luis. *Labyrinths.* Edited by Donald A. Yates and James E. Irby. New York: New Directions Books, 1964.

Burgess, Anthony. *Joysprick: An Introduction to the Language of James Joyce.* New York: Harcourt Brace Jovanovich, 1973.

Butor, Michel. *Mobile: Study for a Representation of the United States (Mobile, 1962).* Translated by Richard Howard. New York: Simon and Schuster, 1963.

Calvino, Italo. "The Implosion." Translated by Eugene Scalia. *Literary Review* 28, 2 (1985): 215–221.

——. *Invisible Cities* (1972). Translated by William Weaver. New York: Harcourt Brace Jovanovich, 1974.

Caproni, Giorgio. "Sure Direction." Translated by Annalisa Sacca. *Literary Review,* 28, 2 (1985): 222.

Carroll, Lewis. *Alice in Wonderland.* New York: New American Library, 1960.

——. *Through the Looking Glass.* New York: New American Library, 1960.

Carter, Angela. *Nights at the Circus.* New York: Penguin Books, 1984.

Cixous, Hélène. *The Exile of James Joyce* (1972). Translated by Sally A. J. Purcell. London: John Calder, 1976.

Cixous, Hélène, and Catherine Clément. *The Newly Born Woman (La jeune née, 1975).* Translated by Betsy Wing. Manchester: Manchester University Press, 1986.

Davenport, Guy. *The Geography of the Imagination.* San Francisco: North Point Press, 1981.

De Lauretis, Teresa. *Technologies of Gender.* Bloomington: Indiana University Press, 1987.

Deleuze, Gilles, and Félix Guattari. *Anti-Oedipus: Capitalism and Schizophrenia* (1972). Translated by Robert Hurley, Mark Seem, and Helen R. Lane. Minneapolis: University of Minnesota Press, 1983.

——. *Kafka: Toward a Minor Literature* (1975). Translated by Dana Polan. Minneapolis: University of Minnesota Press, 1986.

———. *A Thousand Plateaus: Capitalism and Schizophrenia* (1980). Translated by Brian Massumi. Minneapolis: University of Minnesota Press, 1987.

Derrida, Jacques. *Dissemination* (1972). Translated by Barbara Johnson. Chicago: University of Chicago Press, 1981.

———. *Margins of Philosophy* (1972). Translated by Alan Bass. Chicago: University of Chicago Press, 1982.

———. *Of Grammatology* (1967). Translated by Gayatri Chakravorty Spivak. Baltimore: Johns Hopkins University Press, 1976.

———. *Positions* (1972). Translated by Alan Bass. Chicago: University of Chicago Press, 1981.

———. *The Post Card: From Socrates to Freud and Beyond* (1980). Translated by Alan Bass. Chicago: University of Chicago Press, 1987.

Dillard, Annie. *Living by Fiction.* New York: Harper and Row, 1982.

DuPlessis, Rachel Blau. *The Pink Guitar: Writing as Feminist Practice.* New York: Routledge, 1990.

Eisenman, Peter. "Architecture as a Second Language: The Texts of Between." *Threshold* 4 (1988): 71–75.

Eisenstein, Sergei. "Piranesi, or the Fluidity of Forms." Translated by Roberta Reeder. *Oppositions* 11 (1978): 83–110.

Eliot, T. S. *The Waste Land and Other Poems.* New York: Harcourt, Brace and World, 1962.

Evans, Robin. "Translations from Drawing to Building." *AA Files* 12 (1986): 3–18.

Faulkner, William. *Sartoris.* New York: Random House, 1956.

Foucault, Michel. *The Order of Things: An Archaeology of the Human Sciences* (1966). New York: Random House, 1973.

Fraley, David. "Pigeon Coup." Unpublished poems.

Frascari, Marco. "Carlo Scarpa in Magna Graecia: The Abatellis Palace in Palermo." In *AA Files,* number 9, 1985, pp. 3–9.

French, Marilyn. *Beyond Power: On Women, Men, and Morals.* New York: Ballantine Books, 1985.

Gallop, Jane. *Reading Lacan.* Ithaca, N.Y.: Cornell University Press, 1985.

Gilbert, Stuart. *James Joyce's* Ulysses. New York: Vintage Books, 1955.

Hart, Clive. *Structure and Motif in* Finnegans Wake. Evanston: Northwestern University Press, 1962.

Hayman, David, and Elliot Anderson, eds. *In the Wake of the* Wake. Madison: University of Wisconsin Press, 1978.

Hayles, N. Katherine. *Chaos Bound: Orderly Disorder in Contemporary Literature and Science.* Ithaca, N.Y.: Cornell University Press, 1990.

———. *The Cosmic Web: Scientific Field Models and Literary Strategies in the Twentieth Century.* Ithaca, N.Y.: Cornell University Press, 1984.

Heidegger, Martin. *Poetry, Language, Thought.* Translated by Albert Hofstadter. New York: Harper and Row, 1971.

Heraclitus. See Kahn, Charles.

Hersey, George. *The Lost Meaning of Classical Architecture: Speculations on Orna-
    ment from Vitruvius to Venturi.* Cambridge, Mass.: MIT Press, 1989.

hooks, bell. *Yearning: race, gender, and cultural politics.* Boston: South End
    Press, 1990.

Ingraham, Catherine. "The Faults of Architecture: Troping the Proper." *Assemblage*
    7 (1988): 7–13.

———. "Milking Deconstruction, or Cow Was the Show?" *Inland Architect* 32, 5
    (September/October 1988): 61–65.

Irigaray, Luce. *Speculum of the Other Woman* (1974). Translated by Gillian C. Gill.
    Ithaca, N.Y.: Cornell University Press, 1985.

Jameson, Fredric. *The Political Unconscious: Narrative as a Socially Symbolic Act.*
    Ithaca, N.Y.: Cornell University Press, 1981.

———. "Postmodernism, or the Cultural Logic of Late Capitalism." *New Left Review*
    146 (1984): 53–93.

———. *The Prison-House of Language: A Critical Account of Structuralism and
    Russian Formalism.* Princeton, N.J.: Princeton University Press, 1972.

———. "Third-World Literature in the Era of Multinational Capitalism." *Social Text*
    15 (1986) 65–88.

Jardine, Alice A. *Gynesis: Configurations of Woman and Modernity.* Ithaca, N.Y.:
    Cornell University Press, 1985.

Johnson, Barbara. "The Frame of Reference: Poe, Lacan, Derrida." *Yale French
    Studies* 55–56 (1977): 457–505.

Joyce, James. *Finnegans Wake.* New York: Viking Press, 1939.

———. *Ulysses* (1922). New York: Random House, 1961.

Kafka, Franz. *The Penal Colony.* New York: Schocken Books, 1976.

Kahn, Andrea, ed. *Drawing/Building/Text.* Princeton, N.J.: Princeton Architectural
    Press, 1991.

Kahn, Charles. *The Art and Thought of Heraclitus.* Cambridge: Cambridge Univer-
    sity Press, 1983.

Kelley, Donald. "Vico's Road: From Philosophy to Jurisprudence and Back." In
    Giambattista Vico's Science of Humanity, edited by Giorgio Tagliacozzo
    and Donald Phillip Verene, 15–29. Baltimore: Johns Hopkins University
    Press, 1976.

Kimball, Roger. "The Death and Resurrection of Postmodern Architecture." *New
    Criterion,* June 1988, 21–31.

Krauss, Rosalind E. "Sculpture in the Expanded Field." *October* 8 (Spring 1979):
    30–44.

Kristeva, Julia. *Desire in Language: A Semiotic Approach to Literature and Art*
    (1977). Edited by Leon Roudiez; translated by Alice Jardine, Thomas
    Gora, and Leon Roudiez. Oxford: Blackwell, 1980.

———. *Semiotike: recherches pour une semanalyse.* Paris: Seuil, 1969.

Kroker, Arthur, and Marilouise Kroker, eds. *The Hysterical Male: new feminist theory*. Montreal: New World Perspectives, 1991.

Kundera, Milan. *The Unbearable Lightness of Being*. London: Faber and Faber, 1984.

Lacan, Jacques. "Seminar on 'The Purloined Letter.'" Translated by Jeffrey Mehlman. *Yale French Studies* 48 (1972): 38–72.

Laugier, Marc-Antoine. *An Essay on Architecture (Essai sur l'architecture, 1753)*. Translated by Wolfgang Herrmann and Anni Herrmann. Los Angeles: Hennessey and Ingalls, 1977.

Lecercle, Jean-Jacques. *Philosophy through the Looking Glass: Language, nonsense, desire*. London: Hutchinson, 1985.

Leitch, Vincent. *Deconstructive Criticism: An Advanced Introduction*. New York: Columbia University Press, 1983.

Loos, Adolf. *Spoken into the Void*. Translated by Jane O. Newman and John H. Smith. Cambridge, Mass.: MIT Press, 1982.

Lotman, Jurij. *The Semiotics of Cinema*. Translated by Mark E. Suino. Ann Arbor: University of Michigan Department of Slavic Languages and Literature, 1976.

Lynch, Kevin. *The Image of the City*. Cambridge, Mass.: MIT Press, 1960.

Melville, Stephen. "Notes on the Reemergence of Allegory, the Forgetting of Modernism, the Necessity of Rhetoric, and the Conditions of Publicity in Art and Criticism." *October* 19 (1981): 54–92.

Moraga, Cherríe, and Gloria Anzaldúa, eds. *This Bridge Called My Back: Writings by Radical Women of Color*. Watertown, Mass.: Kitchen Table: Women of Color Press, 1981.

Needham, Rodney. Review of Claude Lévi-Strauss' *Le regard éloigné*. *Times Literary Supplement*, 13 April 1984, 393–395.

Norris, Margot. *The Decentered Universe of* Finnegans Wake. Baltimore: Johns Hopkins University Press, 1976.

Ortega y Gasset, José. "On the Point of View in the Arts." Translated by Paul Snodgrass and Joseph Frank. In *The Dehumanization of Art and Other Essays on Art, Culture, and Literature* (1948), 107–130. Princeton, N.J.: Princeton University Press, 1968.

Owens, Craig. "The Allegorical Impulse: Toward a Theory of Postmodernism." *October* 9 (1979): 67–86.

Pérez-Gómez, Alberto. "The Architect's Metier." *Section a* 2, 516 (1985): 26–28.

Phillipson, Michael. *In Modernity's Wake: The Amereunculus Letters*. London: Routledge, 1989.

Potts, Willard. *Portraits of the Artist in Exile*. Seattle: University of Washington Press, 1979.

Pynchon, Thomas. *Gravity's Rainbow*. New York: Bantam Books, 1973.

———. *V*. New York: Bantam Books, 1981.

Ricoeur, Paul. *Time and Narrative,* vol. 1. Translated by Kathleen McLaughlin and
     David Pellauer. Chicago: University of Chicago Press, 1984.

Robinson, Lillian S. "Canon Fathers and Myth Universe." *New Literary History* 19,
     1 (Autumn 1987): 23–35.

Rossi, Aldo. *A Scientific Autobiography.* Translated by Lawrence Venuti. Cambridge:
     MIT Press, 1981.

Said, Edward. *Beginnings: Intention and Method.* New York: Columbia University
     Press, 1985.

Schor, Naomi. *Reading in Detail: Aesthetics and the Feminine.* New York: Methuen,
     1987.

Segrest, Robert. "The Perimeter Projects: The Architecture of the Excluded Middle."
     Perspecta (The Yale Architectural Journal) 23 (1987): 54–65.

Segrest, Robert, and Jennifer Bloomer. "Without Architecture" *Art Papers* 8, 4
     (July-August 1984): i.

Serres, Michel. *Hermes: Literature, Science, Philosophy.* Edited by Josué V. Harari
     and David F. Bell. Baltimore: Johns Hopkins University Press, 1983.

A Short Description of Sir John Soane's Museum. Oxford: University Printing
     House, n.d.

Soja, Edward W. *Postmodern Geographies: The Reassertion of Space in Critical
     Social Theory.* London: Verso, 1989.

Spivak, Gayatri Chakravorty. *In Other Worlds: Essays in Cultural Politics.* New
     York: Methuen, 1987.

Summerson, Sir John. *A New Description of Sir John Soane's Museum.* London:
     Trustees of the Soane Museum, 1977.

Summerson, Sir John, with David Watkin and G.-Tilman Mellinghoff. *John Soane.*
     London: Academy Editions, 1983.

Tafuri, Manfredo. "The Dialectics of the Avant-garde: Piranesi and Eisenstein."
     Translated by Marlene Barsoum and Liviu Dimitriu. *Oppositions* 11
     (Winter 1977): 72–80.

——. *The Sphere and the Labyrinth: Avant-Gardes and Architecture from Pira-
     nesi to the 1970s* (1980). Translated by Pellegrino d'Acierno and Robert
     Connolly. Cambridge, Mass.: MIT Press, 1987.

——. *Theories and History of Architecture* (1976). Translated by Giorgio Verrec-
     chia. New York: Harper and Row, 1980.

Taylor, John. "Mr. In-Between: Deconstructing with Peter Eisenman." *New York,*
     17 October 1988, 46–52.

Taylor, Mark C. *Altarity.* Chicago: University of Chicago Press, 1988.

——. *Tears.* Albany: State University of New York Press, 1990.

Tompkins, Jane. "Me and My Shadow." In *Gender and Theory: Dialogues on Femi-
     nist Criticism,* edited by Linda Kauffman, 121–139. New York: Basil
     Blackwell, 1989.

Tschumi, Bernard. *The Manhattan Transcripts.* London: Academy Editions, 1981.

Ulmer, Gregory. "The Object of Post-Criticism." In *The Anti-Aesthetic: Essays on Postmodern Culture,* edited by Hal Foster, 83–110. Port Townsend, Wash.: Bay Press, 1983.

Vico, Giambattista. *The Autobiography of Giambattista Vico.* Translated by Max Harold Fisch and Tomas Goddard Bergin. Ithaca, N.Y.: Cornell University Press, 1963.

Whiteman, John, Jeffrey Kipnis, and Richard Burdett, eds. *Strategies of Architectural Thinking.* Cambridge, Mass.: MIT Press, 1992.

Wigley, Mark. "Postmortem Architecture: The Taste of Derrida." *Perspecta* (The Yale Architectural Journal) 23 (1987): 156–172.

Wittig, Monique. *Les Guérillères.* Translated by David Levay. London: Women's Press, 1979.

Wolin, Richard. *Walter Benjamin: An Aesthetic of Redemption.* New York: Columbia University Press, 1982.

Yourcenar, Marguerite. *The Dark Brain of Piranesi* (1962). Translated by Richard Howard. New York: Farrar, Straus and Giroux, 1984.

Zukofsky, Louis. *"A."* Garden City, N.J.: Doubleday, 1967; complete ed., Berkeley: University of California Press, 1978.

Illustration Credits

Vesica Piscis. From *Finnegans Wake* by James Joyce. Copyright 1939 by James Joyce, copyright renewed © 1967 by George Joyce and Lucia Joyce. Used by permission of Viking Penguin, a division of Penguin Books.

Rebuses (in text, p. 44). From *Finnegans Wake* by James Joyce. Copyright 1939 by James Joyce, copyright renewed © 1967 by George Joyce and Lucia Joyce. Used by permission of Viking Penguin, a division of Penguin Books.

Illustration of the Trojan Game. Carved drawing on the tragliatella jug. Etruscan, detail. Oldest known illustration of the Trojan game. From the Museo Capitolino, Rome. Photograph used by permission of *Daidalos: Architektur Kunst Kultur.*

Giovanni Battista Piranesi, details from *Il Campo Marzio dell'Antica Roma: Ichnographia.* Etching, six plates. Used by permission of the Fine Arts Library of the University of Pennsylvania.

Giovanni Battista Piranesi, *Plan of an Imaginary Ancient Seat of Learning,* 1750. Etching. 61 × 45 cm (Platemark); 67 × 62 cm (Sheet, trimmed). Gift of Eleanor and Sarah Hewitt, 1931–94–71. Courtesy of the Cooper-Hewitt National Museum of Design, Smithsonian Institution/Art Resource, New York. Photo: Ken Pelka

Giovanni Battista Piranesi, *Le Carceri,* plate 1 (title page), first state (ca. 1745). Used by permission of the Avery Architectural and Fine Arts Library, Columbia University in the City of New York.

Giovanni Battista Piranesi, *Le Carceri,* plate 1 (title page), second state (ca. 1761). Used by permission of the Avery Architectural and Fine Arts Library, Columbia University in the City of New York.

Giovanni Battista Piranesi, *Carcere oscura con Antenna pel Suplizio dé Malfatori.* From *Prima Parte di architettura . . .* , 1743. Used by permission of the Avery Architectural and Fine Arts Library, Columbia University in the City of New York.

Giovanni Battista Piranesi, *Le Carceri,* plate 6 (A Perspective of Arches with a Smoking Fire in the Center), second state (ca. 1761). Used by permission of the Avery Architectural and Fine Arts Library, Columbia University in the City of New York.

Giovanni Battista Piranesi, *Le Carceri,* plate 3 (A Vaulted Building with a Staircase Leading round a Central Column with a Barred Window in the Center), second state (ca. 1761). Used by permission of the Avery Architectural and Fine Arts Library, Columbia University in the City of New York.

Giovanni Battista Piranesi, *Le Carceri,* plate 4 (A Lofty Arch with Vista onto an Arcade Surmounted by a Frieze), second state (ca. 1761). Used by permission of the Avery Architectural and Fine Arts Library, Columbia University in the City of New York.

Superimposition of the *Vesica Piscis* upon the (ideal) façade of Sir John Soane's House and Museum. Drawing by Jennifer Bloomer, after James Joyce in *Finnegans Wake* and Alison Shepherd in Summerson, *John Soane.*

Giovanni Battista Piranesi, *Pianta e Frammenti della Camera sepolcrale esistenie nella Vigna Casali a Porta S. Sebastiano.* Etching, ca. 1754. From the collection of Robert Segrest and Jennifer Bloomer.

Index